SPORTS

FOURTH EDITION

Ferguson
An imprint of Infobase Publishing

Careers in Focus: Sports, Fourth Edition

Copyright © 2008 by Infobase Publishing

Ferguson
An imprint of Infobase Publishing
132 West 31st Street
New York NY 10001

Library of Congress Cataloging-in-Publication Data

Careers in focus. Sports. — 4th ed.
   p. cm.
  Includes bibliographical references and index.
  ISBN-13: 978-0-8160-7287-3 (alk. paper)
  ISBN-10: 0-8160-7287-6 (alk. paper)
  1. Sports—Vocational guidance—Juvenile literature. I. Ferguson Publishing.
II. Title: Sports.
  GV734.3.C38 2008
  796.023—dc22

                        2008028246

Ferguson books are available at special discounts when purchased in bulk quantities for businesses, associations, institutions, or sales promotions. Please call our Special Sales Department in New York at (212) 967-8800 or (800) 322-8755.

You can find Ferguson on the World Wide Web at http://www.fergpubco.com

Text design by David Strelecky
Cover design by Salvatore Luongo

Printed in the United States of America

Sheridan MSRF 10 9 8 7 6 5 4 3 2 1

Table of Contents

Introduction

In the United States, the five major team sports are baseball, basketball, football, hockey, and soccer. All of these sports are structured along much the same general lines. Most sports teams are owned by one person or a number of people. These owners not only pay the salaries of the athletes and other personnel, but they also often exert a strong influence on the personality of a team. Owners may select athletes who appeal to them, and they set rules and regulations that create a particular atmosphere in the clubhouse or locker room. Owners view their teams as businesses, and teams may be bought and sold at the discretion of the owner.

Sports team employees usually work in one of a few major categories. Many work in an administrative capacity in business, management, and consulting offices. Others work as athletes or directly with the athletes, and still others are involved in officiating, sales, concessions, and many other game-day duties.

The media have always been an important part of the sports industry. Newspapers, magazines, television, and the Internet are publicity vehicles for athletes' careers, and live radio and television broadcasts bring the games to large audiences. Today, television has become the dominant financial factor in professional sports.

The sports industry touches on a wide variety of other fields, such as companies that design, manufacture, and sell sporting goods; sports technology manufacturers and maintenance workers; publishing and Internet companies that produce books and Web sites on sports statistics; and advertising and marketing industries that attract your interest to sports and sporting events.

Although team sports are very popular, a wide variety of sports involve very few participants. These sports include tennis, golf, boxing, wrestling, horse racing, running, and race car driving, among others. The structure of these nonteam sports is similar to that of team sports, except rather than being paid by team owners, employees in individual sports may earn money from associations, prize winnings, working for special tours and performances, and from endorsements.

There are more than 150 professional football, baseball, hockey, soccer, and basketball teams on the major league level. This number is relatively stable. This means, however, that the number of jobs is also relatively stable. Job openings for specifically sports-related careers, such as managers, coaches, umpires and referees, occur as people retire or otherwise leave the profession.

As difficult as it is to enter a nonathletic profession, the competition for a job as a professional athlete is much tougher. Out of all of the college athletes who wish to make the pros, very few will be chosen. Of those chosen, many will not last the season; others will not play for more than a couple of years. Few professional football players are able to make a career of the sport, and the same is true for other sports as well. Golf, tennis, and other individual sports enable professionals to play at the international level; however, the financial incentive for players who do not win tournaments is limited.

The U.S. Department of Labor predicts that employment in arts, entertainment, and recreation (which includes the sports industry) will increase by about 25 percent from 2004 to 2014—or 11 percent faster than the growth rate for all industries. Increasing leisure time, the growing interest in amateur and professional sports, and the emergence of new sports leagues and sports (such as extreme sports) are some factors that account for this strong prediction. Careers that will enjoy exceptionally strong employment growth include Sports Trainers, Sports Equipment Managers, Sports Instructors and Coaches, and Groundsmanagers and Groundskeepers.

The sports industry, like sporting events, is very competitive. However, it is potentially a very rewarding field, as well, and not just in terms of salary. After all, many people employed in this industry have been able to make a career out of one of their favorite recreational interests. The articles in this book will help you learn how your education, experience, and interest in sports help you along one of the many career paths in the sports industry.

Each article in *Careers in Focus: Sports* discusses a particular sports occupation in detail. The articles also appear in Ferguson's *Encyclopedia of Careers and Vocational Guidance*—but they have been updated and revised with the latest information from the U.S. Department of Labor and other sources.

The following paragraphs detail the sections and features that appear in the book.

The **Quick Facts** section provides a brief summary of the career including recommended school subjects, personal skills, work environment, minimum educational requirements, salary ranges, certification or licensing requirements, and employment outlook. This section also provides acronyms and identification numbers for the following government classification indexes: the *Dictionary of Occupational Titles* (DOT), the *Guide for Occupational Exploration* (GOE), the National Occupational Classification (NOC) Index, and the Occupational Information Network (O*NET)-Standard

Occupational Classification System (SOC) index. The DOT, GOE, and O*NET-SOC indexes have been created by the U.S. government; the NOC index is Canada's career classification system. Readers can use the identification numbers listed in the Quick Facts section to access further information about a career. Print editions of the DOT (*Dictionary of Occupational Titles*. Indianapolis, Ind.: JIST Works, 1991) and GOE (*Guide for Occupational Exploration*. Indianapolis, Ind.: JIST Works, 2001) are available at libraries. Electronic versions of the NOC (http://www23.hrdc-drhc.gc.ca) and O*NET-SOC (http://online.onetcenter.org) are available on the Internet. When no DOT, GOE, NOC, or O*NET-SOC numbers are present, this means that the U.S. Department of Labor or Human Resources Development Canada have not created a numerical designation for this career. In this instance, you will see the acronym "N/A," or not available.

The **Overview** section is a brief introductory description of the duties and responsibilities involved in this career. Oftentimes, a career may have a variety of job titles. When this is the case, alternative career titles are presented. Employment statistics are also provided, when available. The **History** section describes the history of the particular job as it relates to the overall development of its industry or field. **The Job** describes the primary and secondary duties of the job. **Requirements** discusses high school and postsecondary education and training requirements, any certification or licensing that is necessary, and other personal requirements for success in the job. **Exploring** offers suggestions on how to gain experience in or knowledge of the particular job before making a firm educational and financial commitment. The focus is on what can be done while still in high school (or in the early years of college) to gain a better understanding of the job. The **Employers** section gives an overview of typical places of employment for the job. **Starting Out** discusses the best ways to land that first job, be it through the college career services office, newspaper ads, Internet employment sites, or personal contact. The **Advancement** section describes what kind of career path to expect from the job and how to get there. **Earnings** lists salary ranges and describes the typical fringe benefits. The **Work Environment** section describes the typical surroundings and conditions of employment—whether indoors or outdoors, noisy or quiet, social or independent. Also discussed are typical hours worked, any seasonal fluctuations, and the stresses and strains of the job. The **Outlook** section summarizes the job in terms of the general economy and industry projections. For the most part, Outlook information is obtained from the U.S. Bureau of Labor Statistics and is supplemented by information gathered from professional associations. Job growth terms follow those used in the *Occupational Outlook Handbook*. Growth described as "much faster than the average" means an increase of 27 percent or more. Growth described as "faster than the average" means an increase of 18 to 26 percent. Growth described as "about as fast as the average" means an increase of 9 to 17 percent. Growth described as "more slowly than the average" means an increase of 0 to 8 percent. "Decline" means a decrease by any amount. Each article ends with **For More Information**, which lists organizations that provide information on training, education, internships, scholarships, and job placement.

Careers in Focus: Sports also includes photographs, informative sidebars, and interviews with professionals in the field.

Golf Course Superintendents

OVERVIEW

Golf course superintendents supervise the management and maintenance of the golf course and its associated property, including the golf course and practice areas, golf cart fleet, clubhouse grounds and landscaping, tennis courts, swimming pool, and other recreational facilities, restrooms and potable water on the course, open spaces, wooded areas, and unused acreage. Golf course superintendents supervise the maintenance and repair of machinery and equipment used to maintain the course. They also participate in golf course planning and facility management meetings to advise the management or board of directors on matters regarding the golf course.

HISTORY

Using a bent stick, Roman emperors sent feather-stuffed balls flying through the air in the game, *paganica*. Centuries later in countries throughout Europe, the game had evolved in several variations; the English played *cambuca*, the French played *jeu de mail*, and the Dutch played a version called *het kolven*. The Scottish game *golfe*, however, is the direct ancestor of the modern game. The game became so popular that in 1457, King James II felt he had to ban golfe,

along with *futeball*, in order to guarantee national safety. Apparently, his men were playing the other sports and neglecting their archery skills—which were desperately needed to defend Scotland against the English. The ban was finally removed 45 years later.

In 1744, a group of golfe players in Edinburgh formed the first formal golf club, The Company of Gentleman Golfers (now known as the

Honourable Company of Edinburgh Golfers). The group established standardized rules that were followed until 10 years later when the Royal and Ancient Golf Club of Saint Andrews was created. This club became the official ruling organization of the sport and, along with the United States Golf Association (USGA), still establishes the rules for the sport. The first golf club and course in the United States was the Saint Andrews Golf Club of Yonkers, established in 1888.

Golf is the only major sport in which the playing field does not conform to specific dimensions or characteristics. In fact, the unique natural features of each golf course are what present the golfer with many of the sport's challenges. A golf course generally has 18 holes spread over a landscaped area, called "greens." Courses usually include a number of hazards aimed at making the game more difficult, such as water, rough, trees, and sand traps (also called bunkers). The distance between each hole varies (from 150 to 600 yards), which also increases the difficulty. Play proceeds from hole to hole until golfers have completed the entire 18 holes. Courses vary in speed, uniformity, texture, graininess, and trueness of the greens. The diverse areas of the golf course require that the individuals caring for it have a wide range of knowledge and expertise in everything from plants to ponds.

Scottish tradition affected more than the game. For a long time, secrets of the art of greenskeeping in the United States were passed from one generation of Scotsmen to the next, and it was even believed that a greenskeeper wasn't skilled unless he was Scottish. Today, the greenskeeper has been replaced by the golf course superintendent, but science hasn't completely replaced art in the caring of golf greens. Observation and experience are as valuable to a golf course superintendent as advanced knowledge in science, business, and communications.

THE JOB

Golf course superintendents supervise the management and maintenance of the golf course and its associated property. They interview, hire, train, direct, and supervise a staff of employees including the following: assistant golf course superintendents, equipment managers, assistant equipment mechanics, horticultural technicians, foremen, office assistants, irrigation specialists, chemical technicians, equipment operators, gardeners, and groundskeepers.

Superintendents plan all maintenance and project work and schedule personnel. They routinely inspect and evaluate projects in progress to be sure the facility's standards are met. In addition to supervising the maintenance and repair of machinery and equipment used on the course, superintendents buy or replace equipment and purchase supplies, such as pesticides and fertilizers. They are responsible for inventory and cost control, keeping operating and capital expenses in line with the established budget.

Course superintendents prepare the annual budgets for the care and maintenance of facility and course properties, attend planning meetings, and are called upon to advise the facility's management or board of directors regarding the golf course. They generally report directly to one of the following individuals: the general manager, the greens chairman, the club owner, or the director of parks and recreation. In private club organizations, the superintendent usually must submit plans for course construction, reconstruction, or renovation to the greens committee, but he or she does not need to seek approval for the decisions associated with the everyday maintenance of the course and its properties.

REQUIREMENTS

High School

High school courses that will be helpful to you as a prospective golf course superintendent include business, mathematics, earth science, and agriculture. In addition, speech and English classes will help you communicate effectively with employers and coworkers.

Postsecondary Training

Though not required, golf course superintendents typically hold a degree in agronomy, horticulture, or turfgrass management. "For a high school graduate, the best path to consider is a four-year bachelor's degree," advises Lanie Griffin, career services manager for the Golf Course Superintendents Association of America (GCSAA). "Students who earn these degrees stand a good chance of securing a job in golf course management. Furthermore, today's trend is the higher the level of education achieved, the broader the opportunities and the better the chances for advancement. Whichever program students choose, it should include courses that will help them develop the business and management skills needed for a successful career in golf course management. These include business administration, finance, communications, a foreign language, personnel management, and public relations courses. Students are encouraged to use electives to establish a strong background in business and communications, which will complement agronomic training. Competencies in these areas are essential to a superintendent's professional development."

Agronomy, horticulture, and turfgrass management programs are available at two- and four-year colleges and universities throughout the United States. For a listing, see GCSAA's College Guide at http://www.gcsaa.org.

Certification or Licensing

Many employers prefer to hire course superintendents who are certified by the GCSAA. To be eligible for certification, the candidate must be currently employed as a course superintendent and have a combination of education and experience in the field. They must also submit a portfolio that contains three parts: work samples, skill statements, and case studies. Once a superintendent has been accepted into the GCSAA's program, he or she must pass a comprehensive, six-hour examination that covers the game and rules of golf, turfgrass management, pesticides, environmental considerations, financial management, and human resource management. The certification process includes interviews and course evaluations by two certified superintendents. To pass, both certified superintendents must recommend the candidate. Superintendents must renew their certification every five years by documenting continued participation in a wide range of educational activities.

The Sports Turf Managers Association offers the certified sports field manager designation to applicants who complete education and/or experience requirements and who pass an examination that covers the following subjects: agronomics, pest management, administration, and sports specific field management. This certification is available to all who specialize in turf management, including golf course superintendents.

In addition, golf course superintendents need to be familiar with current federal, state, and local laws and regulations related to golf course management, and when necessary, have the proper state certification or licensing as a pesticide applicator.

Other Requirements

"Professionally," says Lanie Griffin, "a superintendent has to be a good communicator and have the ability to manage people; he/she needs the technical and financial skills necessary to oversee the golf course operation. Knowing the agronomic side of golf is important, but it's equally important to understand the business side of golf. Personally, a superintendent is a hard worker, flexible, and willing to take on challenges, work long hours, and be able to solve problems."

"When we search for golf course superintendents," says Henry DeLozier, vice president of golf for Pulte Homes, a golf course developer, "our top priority is dedication and passion. Next, we look for proven experience. We prefer to hire superintendents who have worked their way up the organization from starter jobs like

Did You Know?

- Golf was first played in Scotland in the 15th century.
- Professional greenskeepers first began caring for golf courses in the 1850s.
- 98 percent of golf course superintendents have completed some post-high school education.
- Four holes of the Brickyard Crossing Golf Course are located in the Indianapolis Motor Speedway. The remaining 14 holes are located outside of the racetrack.
- A properly repaired ball mark will heal in about two to three days. An unrepaired ball mark takes 15 to 20 days to heal.
- The environmental benefits of golf courses include: increased community greenspace; grass, plants, and trees that serve as "air conditioners" that clean the air and create large amounts of oxygen; and turfgrass that traps and holds industrial pollutants.
- The Golf Course Superintendents Association of America was formed in 1926 with 26 members. Today, it has approximately 21,000 members.

Source: Golf Course Superintendents Association of America

weeding and weed-eating through irrigation repair, to chemical application, to personnel management and leadership. But the most important attribute shared by most successful golf course superintendents is the capacity for leadership. A leader must build support and trust in himself/herself. Then, he or she can show the way and teach employees, members, and customers the features and benefits of a great plan. People must first believe in the leader before they embrace the plan."

EXPLORING

Even before you decide on a school or program in turfgrass management, you should try to get firsthand experience in the field to make certain you are entering a career that you enjoy. During high school, activities geared toward plants and turf management are good starting points. Clubs like 4-H and Future Farmers of America sponsor educational programs, activities, and competitions that revolve around horticulture and agronomy. If you are between the ages of five and 22, you might want to join the National Junior Horticultural Association, which offers horticulture-related projects, contests, and other activities. Visit http://www.njha.org for more information.

Even the practical experience of starting and maintaining your own flower or vegetable garden or lawn is something to build on and shows future employers an interest in the field.

A volunteer or part-time job is the next step; begin to build a work history in the field or a related area. Nurseries, public gardens, and parks and recreation offices are involved with the growing and maintenance of flowers and grass. Better yet, apply to the golf course in your area for a position on the groundskeeping crew. No matter how low on the totem pole you may be at first, you have to start somewhere, and, as in most fields, experience counts.

EMPLOYERS

Golf course superintendents are employed by private and public golf courses. Golf is the largest employer of any sport in the United States, with nearly 16,000 courses employing approximately 235,000 workers.

STARTING OUT

Many schools offer internships or cooperative work programs where students in landscape design or turfgrass management can get school credit for working on a golf course. These programs offer participants the chance to gain valuable on-the-job experience, analyze the business and operation of a golf course, and develop personal contacts and future job placement opportunities. Other schools don't offer these sorts of programs, but leave it up to each student to arrange jobs and internships to acquire experience.

If your school doesn't arrange or provide on-the-job training opportunities, applying for work at golf courses after school hours and during the summer is the best option. In the end, graduates with more hands-on experience will have the greatest chance at jobs. Many new graduates believe they will start at the top of the ranks of golf course superintendents. The truth is that nearly all graduates will probably only find positions as assistant golf course superintendents or crew members. After more work, education, and experience are added to their resumes, they can compete for the position of superintendent.

Participating in a GCSAA student chapter at your college or university is a good way to begin valuable networking in the profession and gain information about golf course internships and available scholarships.

ADVANCEMENT

The field of golf course management is increasingly competitive. Obtaining specialized training or advanced education is one way of advancing to top positions. Others advance through on-the-job experience in supervisory positions.

EARNINGS

According to the GCSAA, the average base salary for golf course superintendents was $73,766 in 2006. Superintendents who supervise 18-hole facilities with $1 million–plus budgets earned median salaries of $90,000 annually. GCSAA Class A golf course superintendents, especially those who are certified, earn higher salaries. The average salary of GCSAA Class A superintendents was $78,096 in 2006 and certified golf course superintendents averaged $87,225. At least 14 percent of certified golf course superintendents with bachelor's degrees earned $125,000 or more. Assistant golf course superintendents earned an average of $37,032 in 2006.

WORK ENVIRONMENT

On average, the GCSAA reports that most golf course superintendents' time is divided up as follows: golf course maintenance tasks, 36.4 percent; business management tasks, 28.3 percent; personnel management, 28 percent; and other tasks, 7.3 percent. What keeps them indoors are the numerous management tasks, such as balancing the budget and taking inventory. The rest of their time is spent outdoors, on the course itself, in the nursery, or at other locations on the facilities. Most work year-round, in all kinds of weather, in order to maintain the look of the course. Depending on the geographic location, they may devote more or less time year-round to gardening and grass-cutting duties. For example, the superintendent of a Minnesota course will see his greens under snow for a good portion of the year, while the superintendent of a Florida or Arizona golf course will be managing the greens on his or her course 365 days a year. Which isn't to say that there aren't outdoor tasks during a Minnesota winter; the superintendent is responsible for the health of the trees and plants, as well as the grass. Autumn is spent preparing the grounds and turf for the winter months.

Superintendents work with heavy machinery and chemicals during the maintenance of turf and the application of pesticides. In these instances, they must use caution, following safety guidelines to minimize the risk of an injury.

Golf course superintendents work with a wide variety of people, from those actually playing the game to their maintenance staff working on the courses. Patience and diplomacy are required in order to communicate with guests and staff.

Most golf courses have a greens committee or board of directors. In the case of private country clubs, these boards are usually made up of club members who are nominated to the board for an average period of three years. Board members may have limited understanding of the management of a course; however, they do wield some power as paying club members. As a result, board members' solutions to course management problems may be to fire the superintendent, no matter how unwise a decision that is. Therefore, it is in the best interests of superintendents to develop good negotiating and communication skills. He or she needs to be able to articulate ideas and opinions to the board of directors, and deal firmly with other employees.

OUTLOOK

Although there are nearly 16,000 golf courses in the United States, the number of new golf courses being planned has declined in recent years, according to the GCSAA. As a result, golf course superintendents will face strong employment competition in coming years. Those with experience, strong educational credentials, and a willingness to continuously upgrade their skills throughout their careers will have the best employment prospects. "It is vital that golf course superintendents stay abreast of the ever evolving changes in the business," says Kevin Carroll, general manager/chief operating officer of The Loxahatchee Club in Jupiter, Florida. "From new technology in equipment and agriculture to improved cultural practices, a superintendent must continue learning and educating him/herself and network with other experts in the industry."

FOR MORE INFORMATION

For comprehensive information on golf course management careers, internships, job listings, approved turfgrass management programs, scholarships, membership, and certification, contact
Golf Course Superintendents Association of America
1421 Research Park Drive
Lawrence, KS 66049-3859
Tel: 800-472-7878
Email: infobox@gcsaa.org
http://www.gcsaa.org

For information on internships, scholarships, and certification, contact
Sports Turf Managers Association
805 New Hampshire, Suite E
Lawrence, KS 66044-2774
Tel: 800-323-3875
http://www.stma.org

For articles and developments in the world of golf, visit the following Web site
Royal and Ancient Golf Club of St. Andrews
http://www.randa.org

Groundsmanagers and Groundskeepers

QUICK FACTS

School Subjects
Agriculture
Biology

Personal Skills
Following instructions
Mechanical/manipulative

Work Environment
Primarily outdoors
Primarily multiple locations

Minimum Education Level
Bachelor's degree
  (groundsmanagers)
High school diploma
  (groundskeepers)

Salary Range
$21.87/hour to $27.89/hour
  to $30.59/hour
  (groundsmanagers)
$7.27/hour to $10.22/hour
  to $16.46/hour
  (groundskeepers)

Certification or Licensing
Required for certain positions

Outlook
Faster than the average

DOT
408

GOE
03.01.02

NOC
2225

O*NET-SOC
37-1012.00, 37-1012.02,
  37-3011.00, 37-3012.00,
  37-3013.00

OVERVIEW

Groundsmanagers oversee the maintenance of land and vegetation on sites such as airports, apartment complexes, cemeteries, condominiums, commercial and industrial parks, estates, golf and country clubs, hospitals, military installations, public parks and recreation areas, schools and universities, shopping centers and malls, theme parks, and zoos. They may work alone or supervise a staff of grounds workers. Groundsmanagers may have their own companies or they may work for one or more landscaping companies. Towns, cities, and large sports facilities often have their own grounds management departments and crews.

Groundskeepers are manual laborers who perform a wide variety of tasks related to a site's maintenance, from hauling tree cuttings to mowing lawns. Approximately 1.5 million grounds maintenance workers are currently employed in the United States.

HISTORY

From ancient Egypt to the present, the exterior landscape surrounding public and private buildings has been as important as the interiors of those structures. Water, plants, trees, and flowers (to name a few elements) add beauty, shade, and form to the landscapes outside of our homes and work environments, among many others. The Hanging Gardens of Babylon (circa 600 B.C.), the irrigated

14

gardens at Pasargadae in Persia (sixth century B.C.), and the Romanesque gardens of the Alhambra in Granada (circa A.D. 1377) are all early examples of idyllic settings that, in many ways, have set the standards for landscape designers and groundsmanagers ever since.

Throughout history, gardens served as places to socialize and exercise, as well as to appreciate nature's beauty. Garden styles changed over the years, from the open loggias and terraced gardens of Renaissance Italy; to the great gardens of Andre Le Notre (1613–1700), who aligned windows with garden paths to create the French Classic Style; to the informal, natural forms of English Landscape Style gardens, where lawns and gardens follow the natural lie of the land, rather than imposed geometries.

Frederick Law Olmstead (1822–1903), an American, was the first to use the term *landscape architecture*. In 1858, Olmstead created the first landscaped area in the United States, New York City's Central Park, based on his impressions of the many different gardening styles he saw on his travels in Europe. Today, the influences of the East and West can be found all over the country, from the Japanese-style roof garden of a Manhattan loft building to the Elizabethan herb garden behind an Iowa farmhouse. No matter where the inspiration originated, each garden owes its beauty to the men and women who spend each day pulling weeds, pruning hedges, and planting new cuttings to maintain the integrity of the design and layout.

THE JOB

Groundsmanagers are members of a management team who are responsible for the maintenance of a wide variety of public and private sites. Working under the supervision of groundsmanagers is a crew of groundskeepers, unskilled laborers who work to maintain a site's appearance.

Within the sports industry, groundsmanagers and their crews work to maintain the condition of playing fields of all different types and the lands surrounding the related facilities. For example, groundsmanagers and groundskeepers are hired to keep both natural and artificial turf areas in top condition for the sport played on it. In addition to planting the proper type of natural turf or laying artificial turf and ensuring it has excellent drainage, grounds workers regularly mow, fertilize, and aerate the fields. They spray protective pesticides on natural turf to control weeds, kill pests, and prevent diseases or insect infestations from destroying the field's appearance.

Even artificial turf requires special care; groundsmanagers and their crews must vacuum and disinfect it after a sporting event so that harmful bacteria won't grow and destroy the turf or harm the players who compete on the field. Periodically, the cushioning pad beneath the artificial turf must be replaced. Part of the care for the playing fields includes painting the appropriate boundaries, markers, and team logos and names on the turf, and even retouching them during sporting events.

Groundsmanagers and groundskeepers also maintain the ornamental grasses, shrubs, plants, and flowers on the grounds of a football stadium, baseball park, or general sports arena.

In addition to the "green" side of the job, groundsmanagers fulfill specific supervisory duties, such as managing finances, materials, equipment, and staff needed to maintain a playing field and related facilities. For most managers, this means developing goals, scheduling maintenance operations, assigning staff hours, creating budgets, delegating tasks, conducting cost accounting procedures, and hiring, training, and supervising employees.

Golf is the only major sport in which the playing field does not conform to specific dimensions or characteristics. In fact, the varying natural features of each course present the golfer with many of the sport's challenges. As a result, the diverse areas of the golf course require that the individuals caring for it have a wide range of knowledge and expertise in everything from plants to ponds. The groundskeeper working for a golf course performs routine manual labor related to the care of the grass and shrubs, including operating mowers and string trimmers.

Grounds workers implement the designs of landscape architects and designers and then maintain those designs throughout the year. In general, this means they are responsible for planting, pruning, mowing, transplanting, fertilizing, spraying, trimming, training, edging, and any other duties that will keep the landscape looking healthy and attractive. They may work year-round to ensure the quality of the playing fields and other grounds. Depending upon the region of the country, the groundsmanager might hire extra groundskeepers during peak periods and cut staff during slower months. In general, spring and summer are the peak seasons, while autumn and winter are much slower. However, schedules depend on the site where groundsmanagers and groundskeepers work. For example, fall and winter are the busiest times of the year for the grounds workers who maintain the field of a National Football League team.

REQUIREMENTS

High School

There are no formal educational requirements for becoming a groundskeeper. Groundsmanagers must have a solid education background to prepare them for a college program. While in high school, study chemistry, biology, and earth science, as well as English, foreign languages, and mathematics. Managers need solid communication skills to work well with their crews and need mathematical ability to balance their budgets and keep other records.

Postsecondary Training

Those interested in becoming groundsmanagers should aim for a bachelor of science in groundsmanagement, horticulture, agronomy, or a related field. In addition, most employers require that managers have a minimum of four years of experience, at least two in a supervisory position. Groundsmanagers need to be familiar and comfortable with budgeting, management, and cost-accounting procedures, possess public relations and communication skills, and be current with maintenance issues, such as recycling and hazardous materials. Courses in business management and personnel management are very helpful, although not required.

Most groundskeeping jobs do not require a college degree. Many people working these jobs are either looking to get on-the-job experience or simply trying to make a little extra money. However, some positions involving the application of pesticides, fungicides, and other chemicals do require some educational training.

Certification or Licensing

Grounds professionals who specialize in golf course management can be certified by the Golf Course Superintendents Association of America (GCSAA). To be eligible for certification, the candidate must be currently employed as a course superintendent and have a combination of education and experience in the field. They must also submit a portfolio that contains three parts: work samples, skill statements, and case studies. Once a superintendent has been accepted into the GCSAA's program, he or she must pass a comprehensive, six-hour examination that covers the game and rules of golf, turfgrass management, pesticides, environmental considerations, financial management, and human resource management. The certification process includes interviews and course evaluations by two certified superintendents. To pass, both certified superintendents must recommend the candidate.

The Professional Grounds Management Society offers certification for both groundsmanagers and workers: the certified grounds manager (CGM) certification and the certified grounds technician (CGT) certification. To be eligible to take the CGM exam, candidates must fulfill one of the following requirements: a bachelor of science degree in a recognized industry field and four years of work in the field of grounds maintenance (including two years of supervisory experience); a two-year degree from a recognized college or junior college and six years of work in the field (including three years of supervisory experience); or eight years in the grounds maintenance field with a minimum of four years of supervisory experience. To take the CGT exam, candidates must have a high school diploma or GED and two years of groundskeeping experience.

The Professional Lawn Care Association of America offers the following designations to applicants who pass examinations: certified landscape professional; certified ornamental landscape professional; certified turfgrass professional; certified turfgrass professional, cool season lawns; certified landscape technician, interior; and certified landscape technician, exterior.

The Sports Turf Managers Association offers the certified sports field manager certification to applicants who meet education and/or experience requirements and pass an examination that covers agronomics, pest management, administration, and sports specific field management.

In the interest of public safety, some states require grounds workers to pass a certification examination on the proper application of pesticides, fungicides, and other harsh chemicals.

Other Requirements

To be a successful groundsmanager, you should have good organizational, communication, and leadership skills, and be able to work under deadline pressure. Groundskeepers must be able to follow directions and be responsible, since they are often assigned duties and then asked to work without direct supervision.

EXPLORING

If you are between the ages of five and 22, you might consider joining the National Junior Horticultural Association, which offers horticulture-related projects, contests, and other activities. Visit http://www.njha.org for more information.

Groundskeeping positions are excellent entry-level jobs for high school students looking to gain valuable experience. Prior work in a grounds crew can help you later when you are pursuing a career in grounds management. Because most groundskeeping positions are seasonal, you can work part-time after school and on weekends during the school year and full-time during the summer. Interested students should start by contacting the municipal parks district, lawn care companies, nurseries, botanical gardens, and professional landscapers in their area to inquire about job possibilities.

EMPLOYERS

There are approximately 1.5 million grounds workers currently employed in the United States. Managers and supervisors hold 184,000 jobs; groundskeepers hold approximately 1.17 million jobs. Grounds workers are employed at golf and country clubs, public parks and recreation areas, apartment complexes, cemeteries, condominiums, estates, schools and universities, shopping centers and malls, theme parks, zoos, commercial and industrial parks, hospitals, airports, and military installations. Cities, towns, and sporting facilities also employ their own groundsmanagement workers. Groundsmanagers may have their own business or work for one or more landscaping companies.

STARTING OUT

Depending on their experience prior to receiving a degree in agronomy or horticulture, candidates for management positions can start in an entry-level groundskeeping job. Working in a nursery, botanical garden, or park offers the opportunity to learn about the care of plants, flowers, trees, and shrubs. A summer job may evolve into a full-time supervisory position following graduation from a four-year program.

ADVANCEMENT

Advancement usually comes with increased expertise from on-the-job experience (especially in a supervisory position) and additional courses in botany, agronomy, horticulture, and pesticide application. Two- and four-year programs in grounds management, landscape management, turfgrass management, and ornamental horticulture are widely available.

Groundskeepers who acquire additional education and experience can easily advance into management positions. Even a two-year degree can help accelerate a groundskeeper into supervisory jobs.

EARNINGS

Salaries for groundsmanagers vary depending on level of education, training, and experience. According to a survey by the Professional Grounds Management Society, the average hourly salary for managers/superintendents was $27.89 in 2004. Salaries ranged from a low of $21.87 to $30.59 an hour.

By comparison, the hourly wages for groundskeepers are much lower. Most groundskeepers only earned between $8.38 and $12.91

an hour (or roughly $17,430 to $26,860 a year) in 2006. The most experienced groundskeepers earned $16.46 or more an hour, or $34,240 or more a year. The low wages are one reason why these jobs are often hard to keep filled, with groundskeeping staff continually leaving to find better-paying work.

The *Chicago Tribune* reports that earnings for groundskeepers employed with a sports team to care for the home stadium are much higher. In 2000, the head groundskeeper for the Chicago White Sox reported earning between $45,000 and $110,000 a year. However, he also reported working up to 110-hour weeks when the Sox were in town!

WORK ENVIRONMENT

For both managerial and nonmanagerial positions, the work is physically demanding, although perhaps more so for groundskeepers. They shovel dirt, haul branches and other cuttings, move large rocks, and dig holes. Groundsmanagers and groundskeeping crews work outside year-round, in all types and conditions of weather. Management positions, in general, tend to be full-time and, as such, are not affected by the seasons. Some portion of a groundsmanager's day is spent taking care of administrative duties inside an office. Groundsmanagers may need to schedule their workers' weekly hours, compute their wages, order chemicals and other supplies, and inventory the tools.

On the other hand, groundskeepers spend nearly all of their day outside, performing primarily manual labor. Groundskeeping jobs, unlike grounds management positions, are seasonal and tied to the heavy demands of spring and summer planting, trimming, and mowing. Landscapers and other employers of groundskeeping crews usually need more staff members during these peak periods and may not promise year-round employment. In more temperate climates, however, such as Florida or Southern California, there is no shortage of year-round jobs.

Groundsmanagers and groundskeepers for sports facilities are usually under a lot of pressure to complete a job in time for a sports event, and often these sports events are televised, making it that much more important that the football field or baseball diamond looks well cared for.

Pesticides, herbicides, and fungicides are necessary to keep turf, plants, shrubs, trees, and flowers healthy and beautiful. Groundsmanagers and their crews frequently work with these and other chemicals, and it is essential that they observe safety precautions when applying these chemicals to prevent exposure. Similarly, grounds-managers and their crews use many different tools and machines to complete their tasks, from driving a truck or lawn mower, to operating power clippers, chain saws, and sod cutters.

OUTLOOK

The U.S. Department of Labor reports that the employment of groundskeeping workers will grow faster than the average for all occupations through 2014. Growth is expected in the construction of commercial and industrial buildings, homes, highways, and recreational facilities, which will require grounds maintenance professionals to tend to the general landscaping. Homeowners increasingly rely on landscaping services to maintain the beauty and value of their property. The demand for parks and recreational facilities also can be expected to create demand for grounds maintenance workers. In addition, a high turnover rate, especially among the groundskeeping occupations, offers many opportunities for employment.

Professional sports arenas, stadiums, and fields and the athletes who play in these venues generate billions of dollars. The appearance of a playing field is extremely important to the team and the community that supports it. Fans and sports management alike take great pride in the way their baseball stadium looks, for example, when it is televised in a national broadcast. Groundsmanagers and their crews will always remain a vital part of maintaining a sports team's image.

FOR MORE INFORMATION

For information on horticultural education, careers, and scholarships, contact
American Society for Horticultural Science
113 South West Street, Suite 200
Alexandria, VA 22314-2851
Tel: 703-836-4606
http://www.ashs.org

For comprehensive information on golf course management careers, internships, job listings, approved turfgrass management programs, and certification, contact
Golf Course Superintendents Association of America
1421 Research Park Drive
Lawrence, KS 66049-3859

Tel: 800-472-7878
Email: infobox@gcsaa.org
http://www.gcsaa.org

For information on student membership and certification, contact
Professional Grounds Management Society
720 Light Street
Baltimore, MD 21230-3816
Tel: 800-609-7467
Email: pgms@assnhqtrs.com
http://www.pgms.org

For information on certification, careers, internships, and student membership, contact
Professional Landcare Network
950 Herndon Parkway, Suite 450
Herndon, VA 20170-5528
Tel: 800-395-2522
http://www.landcarenetwork.org/cms/home.html

For information on internships, scholarships, and certification, contact
Sports Turf Managers Association
805 New Hampshire, Suite E
Lawrence, KS 66044-2774
Tel: 800-323-3875
http://www.sportsturfmanager.org

For profiles of professionals working in a variety of careers, visit
enPlant: Horticulture & Crop Science in Virtual Perspective
http://enplant.osu.edu/index.lasso

For online information on the industry, career leads, and other resources, visit the following Web site:
Landscape Management
http://www.landscapemanagement.net

Jockeys

OVERVIEW

Jockeys train and ride thoroughbred horses in professional competitions. They exercise the horses by galloping and working them throughout the day. Along with the horse's owner and trainer, the jockey prepares his or her horse for competition by working to improve the horse's specific racing strengths and, if possible, rid the horse of its weaknesses. In Quarter Horse and obstacle racing, the horses are guided by riders. *Drivers* sit in special carts in harness racing, using the reins to steer their horses to victory. There are approximately 1,500 professional jockeys employed in the United States.

HISTORY

Historically used for work and transportation, horses have been in use since 2000 B.C. when they were introduced in Babylonia and then in Egypt. Horse racing itself is one of the oldest sports and among the most popular today. The Greeks built courses called *hippodromes* for horse and chariot racing, which eventually became events in the ancient Olympic games. Modern racing originated in England about the 12th century, when monarchs and noblemen first began importing foreign breeds renowned for their stamina and speed. Matching the fastest horses became popular at country fairs, and the first public racetrack was built in London in 1174. Today, the term *horse racing* refers to organized racing at licensed tracks or courses. There are four types of racing: thoroughbred, harness, Quarter Horse, and obstacle. In harness racing, the horses pull carts with drivers; in all other types of racing, the horses are ridden by jockeys, or riders.

Thoroughbred racing, in which all of the horses are of the Thoroughbred breed, is the most popular type of horse racing. The Thoroughbred breed, developed in England in the 18th century, is made up of three stallions—the Byerly Turk, Darley Arabian, and Godolphin Barb—that were originally imported to England and chosen as the founding sires of the breed because of their speed and stamina. In order to compete, the horses must be at least two years old.

In its earliest form, American racing was conducted in much the same fashion as English racing; horses were raced on a grassy surface, in a clockwise direction. Eventually, Americans altered the sport, adopting counterclockwise racing and dirt surfaces. The first dirt racetrack was a course created in 1821 in New York. Today, all American races are run counterclockwise on oval-shaped courses. Only 5 percent of all races are not run on dirt courses. In addition to dirt racetracks, approximately 40 percent of all American racetracks have a turf course, as well.

The actual racing oval ranges in size from five-eighths of a mile to one-and-a-half miles. Most racing ovals are one mile in circumference. The track is marked off in *furlongs,* or eighths of a mile.

Racing is conducted year-round across the United States, with nearly 100 racetracks in operation. Most tracks conduct racing for one or more meets during the year. A meet may last anywhere from a few days to several months. There may be as many as 10 races per day. In those states that have more than one racetrack, the meets are scheduled so they do not overlap. Careful scheduling enables trainers to move their horses among several different tracks and provides more opportunities for a continual season of racing.

In the United States, the best-known races are the Kentucky Derby (Louisville), Preakness Stakes (Baltimore), and Belmont Stakes (Long Island). A horse that accomplishes the rare feat of winning all three races in one year is the winner of the Triple Crown. Triple Crown winners of the past include Gallant Fox (1930), War Admiral (1937), Whirlaway (1941), Citation (1948), Secretariat (1973), and Affirmed (1978). Among the greatest jockeys are Eddie Arcaro and Willie Shoemaker.

THE JOB

Jockeys ride Thoroughbred racehorses on the horse racing circuit. It is the jockey's job to guide his or her horse, or mount, through the horse traffic on the way to the finish line. Years of hard work, practice, and racing experience can teach a jockey how to successfully move the horse through the crowd, but there is no substitute for instinct and daring. Split-second timing and quick reflexes are also among the necessary qualities. Jockeys work with trainers, grooms, and exercisers to develop the horses for racing. Special exercises or drills focus on building the horse's stamina for longer races or developing a final "kick" or spurt of speed for the finish of a race. Trainers and jockeys also run the horse through time trials, pushing the horse through several mock races in the same way a sprinter or long distance runner practices by running a series of sprints or taking different routes of varied distances.

In addition to working on the horse and its skills, many jockeys submit their bodies to tough workouts in the gym. Being in good shape is crucial for many reasons. A jockey's weight is important because the lighter the rider, the less burdened the horse is by the added weight and the faster the horse may be able to run. However, lightness alone is not worth much without the requisite strength and skill to control powerful, often spirited horses. The successful jockey is in excellent physical condition, has quick reflexes, and has a good "touch" with the riding crop. In addition to working out the horses and working out in the gym, jockeys study films in order to see their mistakes and learn techniques from more experienced riders. Every race is photographed, filmed, or captured on video, primarily as a safeguard. If a jockey feels another horse illegally passed or moved up, he or she can have the race finish questioned. However, the films and videos are instructive, too. The races are shot from many different angles, and young riders can learn about race riding by picking up tactics and strategies from the films. Jockeys help each other. If a young jockey shows interest and the willingness to listen, he or she will be rewarded by the advice of older, more experienced jockeys.

Many jockeys work as independent contractors who ride for different barns, trainers, and owners. A specific barn may hire a good jockey for a whole season because that jockey works well with a certain horse. Generally, jockeys have fairly stable working hours during racing season. Their days usually begin early in the morning and end in the early evening after a long day of racing.

On race day, each jockey wears breeches, boots, cap, and a colorful blouse in the special colors of the horse's owner. These colorful shirts are made from silk and, for that reason, are known as the jockey's *silks*.

Before each race, jockeys are weighed with their saddles so that track officials can be certain each horse is carrying its assigned weight. Racing saddles usually weigh around two pounds. Horses are saddled in the paddock, an enclosed area off the track. The jockeys mount their horses and are then summoned by a bugle call to begin moving to the starting gate, or *post*. The horses must move in a single-file line toward the post; this is known as *the parade to the post.* Because the number of horses in any race may vary from as few as five to as many as 20, the jockey must be able to handle his or her horse around other horses, especially when the horse becomes distracted or nervous.

The race begins when all of the horses and jockeys are in position within the individual stalls in the starting gate. The official race starter presses a button that rings a bell and opens the gate, and the horses charge out. During the race, the jockeys must utilize their quick reflexes and knowledge of pace to make split-second decisions. Their goal is to continually better their horse's position among the other horses, or the *field,* by making strategic, well-timed, and legal moves and passes. Some horses naturally have a particular style, such as a strong finish, and it is up to the jockey to manage or shape that style into a *win, place,* or *show* finish—first, second, and third, respectively.

The winning jockey is weighed again after the race, and his or her horse is tested for the presence of illegal drugs. In photo-finish races, stewards, or judges, determine the winner by studying photographs or video of the race finish. A tie is referred to in the industry as a *dead heat.*

If a rider believes he or she was fouled by another horse and rider (by being bumped or prevented from passing in an illegal manner, for example), he or she may go to the race stewards and claim a foul. The stewards then examine any camera footage they have available to them and make a ruling as to whether or not the horse (and rider) will be disqualified. Following a race, jockeys spend several hours studying films of their race to improve their technique and study the strengths and weaknesses of the competition.

REQUIREMENTS
High School
There are no specific educational requirements for becoming a jockey. There are riding schools for jockeys, but most jockeys get their training by immersing themselves in the world of horse racing and learning the basics while performing support tasks such as exercising and training horses. In high school, your best bet is to get a well-rounded education. Classes in physical education will build your strength and agility, while business courses will give you a general working knowledge of finances and money management—skills you will need when you become a jockey.

Other Requirements
Jockeys must be at least 16 years old. There is no set height or weight requirement, but the majority of jockeys do not weigh more than 125

pounds, many even less, with height (usually around 5 feet tall) proportionate to their weight. A jockey should be daring, mentally alert, scrupulously honest, and an excellent judge of pace. Most importantly, a jockey needs to understand and be familiar with horses. It is not enough to be simply a good rider. Part of knowing when to move your horse into position during a race is simply knowing your horse. The best way to get this experience is to spend as much time as possible on and around horses.

Jockeys are outstanding riders. They must be able to cope with a nervous, frightened, or high-spirited horse. And because the weather on a race day is never predictable, jockeys need to be able to "read" the track through a driving rain or on a dry and dusty day.

Finally, jockeys must abide by the rules of the sport, as determined by the racing commission of the county or state in which they are racing. These rules differ from state to state (although an effort is being made by the Association of Racing Commissioners International to standardize the rules), and it is up to the jockeys and their managers to make certain that the jockeys do not violate any of them. For example, a jockey and his or her mount might be disqualified if the jockey wore the wrong silks during the race. The racing commission makes rulings on such things as interference, horse whipping, and proper headgear.

EXPLORING

Anyone interested in a career with horses should first get used to being around them. Volunteer at a stable or take riding lessons. Some stables need part-time and full-time help, depending on the season and location. Many larger facilities offer positions where you may clean stalls, feed and groom horses, and maintain stables. 4-H is also a good place for you to get involved with the care, grooming, and sport of horses.

EMPLOYERS

Many jockeys work as independent contractors who ride for different barns, trainers, and owners. There are nearly 100 racetracks located throughout the United States.

STARTING OUT

Most jockeys begin their careers by riding whenever they can, sometimes by living with or working part time for a licensed owner or trainer who supervises young riders. The student must be willing to learn the business from the bottom up, including cleaning out stalls, caring for saddles, halters, bridles and other equipment, cooling down hot horses after they have been worked out, and performing any number of similar tasks.

The next step is to work at the job of exercising horses. Most jockeys get their start by working as *horse exercisers* for early morning workouts that include galloping, working, and cooling out horses. Horse exercisers warm up the horse, moving the horse through a variety of drills to raise the horse's temperature to a level where the chance of injury is lessened. This process is similar to the warm-up that a human athlete does to warm up his or her muscles before a strenuous workout. Exercisers also cool out the horse, gradually reducing the animal's heart rate by slowing down the horse to a slow walk, for example. This technique corresponds to the athlete who stretches his or her muscles following a workout.

Working as an exerciser also gets the potential jockey in good physical shape and develops his or her feel for a horse and its capabilities. Afterwards, the trainer and jockey work with the horse, and the exerciser either moves on to another horse or is able to watch and learn from the experienced jockey. As the exerciser gains experience, he or she moves on to a position as an apprentice rider. This training period usually takes one to three years.

When the owner or trainer feels the student is ready to ride in a race, he or she places the student under written contract to ride as an apprentice rider. The contract made between employer and apprentice jockey is binding throughout the world of horseracing. Both parties must live up to the conditions of the agreement, and the contract can only be voided by mutual consent or upon proof of serious grievance to the racing stewards.

Because the training weight is lower for apprentice riders, owners like to have them ride their horses early on, to clock fast times. This also helps the apprentice rider gain experience. Apprentice riders race for their trainer or owner, building up their reputations as jockeys until an agent notices them. With or without an agent, the apprentice rider tries to participate in as many races as possible. Agents usually notice young talents and try to sign them. A good agent can increase the number of mounts and help improve the young jockey's reputation among owners and trainers.

ADVANCEMENT

As a jockey begins to win races and establish a reputation for solid riding and good instincts, opportunities will increase to ride the

Jockeys must be outstanding riders. During a race, they should be daring, mentally alert, and excellent judges of pace. *(Seth Joel, Corbis)*

more renowned horses of prestigious owners. The better the horse, the better the jockey's chances for winning and the greater the increase in the jockey's earnings. Prize thoroughbreds race for millions of dollars, and the jockey who rides a horse to a first place finish in one of the major races will be sought after by both trainers and owners.

There are only about 1,500 jockeys riding in the United States, and of that number only a few will reach the position of independence that comes with championship-caliber riding. Moderate success, however, can still be very rewarding for the individual who truly loves the sport.

Some jockeys may move into the field of training or, eventually, when they can no longer ride, buy a horse and train it for someone else to ride. Owning and managing a thoroughbred racehorse is expensive, however; without partners or outside funds, this can be difficult.

EARNINGS

Although some jockeys have won purses in the million-dollar range, even the highest-paid jockeys in America earn less than the top performers in other sports. The earnings of the 50 top jockeys in 2006 ranged from $2,793,626 to $20,122,592, according to Equibase Company LLC. Generally, jockeys receive a percentage of the purse or overall winnings of a race. For example, if a purse is $3,000, a jockey may get 10 percent, or $300. Purses depend on the track where a race is being held. A few purses are for as much as $1 million, although these are exceptions, according to the Jockeys' Guild. The most lucrative races are in Kentucky, California, and New York.

All this means is that after the sound of the cheering crowds has died down, the winning jockey can't just take home his or her winnings. In addition to having to pay any travel expenses not covered through the agreement with the owner whose horse he or she rides, the jockey must pay out to his or her agent and valet a certain, predetermined amount.

WORK ENVIRONMENT

Because of the size requirements, very few riders are actually small and strong enough to pursue a professional career as a jockey and, among those who do meet the size requirements, the competition is keen for the top horses. Also, vast sums of money are often riding on the outcome of a particular race. As a result, the jockey faces a great deal of on-the-job stress and pressure. It is one thing knowing that you placed a dollar bet on a particular race; it is quite another thing to know that your employer has placed a bet worth millions.

The horse is a huge part of the equation. Jockeys must spend hours and hours around the horses they ride, caring for and grooming them, in addition to riding them. Depending on the weather, most of the day is spent at a track, working with the trainer and timing the horse in trial runs. At every stage of a jockey's career, long hours and grueling workouts with horses are necessary to build and maintain the requisite racing skills. Until they can earn enough to support themselves full time, many aspiring jockeys continue to work as horse trainers or exercisers, which may seem frustrating. A jockey may also have to travel quite a bit to gain enough experience to work in one place for a season. This may make having a fulfilling private life a bit difficult.

OUTLOOK

In the last few decades, horse events have come to rival other sports as a recreational pursuit, although fewer gambling dollars are available since horse racing now has to compete with other forms of legalized gambling such as lotteries, casino gambling, sports betting, and river boat gambling.

Fewer jobs will be available in the horse industry in coming years since the industry has been on the decline since the mid-1980s. A recession, revised tax laws, and competition with other sports and forms of gambling have taken dollars away from the industry, which had seen steady growth since the 1960s.

FOR MORE INFORMATION

For information on thoroughbred racing, contact
The Jockey Club
40 East 52nd Street
New York, NY 10022-5911
Tel: 212-371-5970
http://www.jockeyclub.com

The Jockeys' Guild is a labor organization designed to improve the working conditions of jockeys. For more information, contact
Jockeys' Guild
PO Box 150
Monrovia, CA 91017-0150
Tel: 866-GO-JOCKS
Email: info@jockeysguild.com
http://www.jockeysguild.com

For general information about the thoroughbred racing industry, visit
Equine Line
http://www.equineline.com

Professional Athletes— Individual Sports

OVERVIEW

In contrast with amateur athletes who play or compete in amateur circles for titles or trophies only, *professional athletes* participate in individual sports such as tennis, figure skating, golf, running, or boxing, competing against others to win prizes and money.

HISTORY

The origin of the first recreational activity—or sport—is not known. It can be assumed, however, that the notion of sport was born the first time anyone attempted to fish, hunt, or wrestle, simply for the pleasure of it or to compete against another person, rather than for self-preservation. Wrestling matches, for example, are believed to have taken place 5,000 years ago in ancient Sumeria; archeological excavations there turned up cave drawings depicting men wrestling one another while others looked on. Like the skills associated with hunting and fishing, wrestling and other hand-to-hand combat skills were developed in order to survive. Competitions to see who had the best skills in these areas inevitably resulted in a love of and devotion to the skill, or sport, itself.

The Olympic Games are generally credited as being the first instance of organized sports. Historians believe that they actually began as early as two centuries before the first written mention of them in 776 B.C. Rome's conquest of ancient Greece didn't bring the fabled games to a halt, but instead, the Romans added their own brand of sport to the list, including chariot-racing and gladiator battles. They built special arenas in which to stage these events, from the amphitheater to the renowned Colosseum in Rome. In A.D. 394, however, the Olympic Games were abolished and were not revived until 1896.

In the interim, popular support for organized sports developed slowly. Tennis rose to popularity in France in the 1400s; historical records indicate that a track-and-field competition was held in England in 1510; Mary, Queen of Scots, loved to play golf and popularized the sport during her reign from 1542 to 1567. Her son, James I of England, lifted a ban on football (now known to Americans as soccer). The first sweepstakes in horse racing was introduced in England in 1714.

The difference in the nature of sports before and after the 19th century largely has to do with organization. Prior to the 19th century, most sports were not officially organized; there were no official rules, competitions, or standards of play. During the 19th century, however, many sports underwent a transition from invented pastime to official sport. Rules governing play, the field of play, and competitions were agreed upon. The first modern track-and-field meet, for example, was held in England in 1825. Meanwhile, in the United States the English game of rugby evolved into American football. The first game was played between Rutgers and Princeton in 1869.

Baseball, basketball, golf, tennis, and then boxing began to attract large crowds of people in the years before World War II. As these sports and others grew in popularity, governing bodies and organizations were created to oversee the fair play of each sport. Gradually, coverage of sporting events on radio and in newspapers began to grow until sports quite literally became the national pastime for Americans. Sports stars became as renowned as movie stars or politicians, sometimes even more so.

Sports, both individual and team, have often provided the first opportunity to break political and social prejudices. At the 1936 Olympic Games in Berlin, before a primarily German crowd that included Adolph Hitler, an African American, Jesse Owens, won the 100-yard dash; won the long-jump and set a record that stood for 25 years; won the 220-yard dash and 220-yard low hurdles; and was a member of the winning 4 x 100-yard relay team, which Hitler had previously predicted would be a showcase for Aryan supremacy. Until the 1940s, professional sports remained segregated in the United States, with occasional exceptions in boxing and track and field. In 1947, Jackie Robinson broke racial lines when the Brooklyn Dodgers signed him.

Today the number of professional team sports is growing, but the numbers still favor male athletes. Only a few professional teams exist for female athletes, none of which are currently promoted or supported by the media and public to the degree that male teams are. Professional sports have long remained closed to women athletes for a number of reasons, from outright prejudice to finances. For centuries women weren't allowed to exercise strenuously or play a sport, much less devote the time necessary to excelling in a specific sport. It was simply believed to be unappealing and unseemly for a woman to exert herself. The bias against women in sports went so far as to question the femininity of female athletes.

Women first made their entree into the sports world in individual sports, such as golf (Babe Didrikson Zaharias) and tennis (Suzanne Lenglen). These two women alone established standards for both male and female athletes. Didrikson Zaharias is considered the greatest woman athlete of the first half of the 20th century. At 16, she was named an All-American high school basketball player, and then proceeded to international fame in track and field, winning several U.S. titles and, in the 1932 Olympic Games, gold medals in the javelin and 80-meter hurdles, and a silver in the high jump. She became a professional golfer in 1948 after great success as an amateur. That year she captured the U.S. Women's Open title, which she won again in 1950 and 1954. Didrikson Zaharias was the Associated Press Woman Athlete of the Year in 1932, 1945–47, 1950, and 1954. Lenglen, who lost only one match between 1919 and 1926 and who won Wimbledon's single's title a record six times, was also the first tennis player to ever sign a contract and undertake a professional tour, which she did in 1926.

The success of these women did not necessarily pave the way for more women—the road would continue to be rough—but their presence in the world of sports certainly made admittance to it for other women a little easier. The stunning play of tennis stars Margaret Court Smith, Billie Jean King, Martina Navratilova, Chris Evert, Venus Williams, and Serena Williams as well as golfers Kathy Whitworth, Nancy Lopez, JoAnne Carner, Pat Bradley, Amy Alcott, and Annika Sorenstam proves that women athletes can excel and entertain as well as their male counterparts.

Today, athletes who compete in individual sports at the professional level earn hundreds of thousands of dollars in salaries or prize money at professional competitions. The top players or athletes in each individual sport earn as much or more in endorsements and advertising, usually for sports-related products and services, but increasingly for products or services completely unrelated to their sport.

THE JOB

Professional athletes participate in individual sports such as tennis, figure skating, golf, running, or boxing, competing against others to win prizes and money.

Depending on the nature of the specific sport, most athletes compete against a field of individuals. The field of competitors can be as small as one (tennis, boxing) or as large as the number of qualified competitors, anywhere from six to 30 (figure skating, golf, cycling). In certain individual events, such as the marathon or triathlon, the field may seem excessively large—often tens of thousands of runners compete in the New York Marathon—but for the professional runners competing in the race, only a handful of other runners represent real competition.

The athletic performances of those in individual sports are evaluated according to the nature and rules of each specific sport. For example, the winner of a foot race is whoever crosses the finish line first; in tennis, the winner is the one who scores the highest in a set number of games; in boxing and figure skating, the winners are determined by a panel of judges. Competitions are organized by local, regional, national, and international organizations and associations whose primary functions are to promote the sport and sponsor competitive events. Within a professional sport there are usually different levels of competition based on age, ability, and gender. There are often different designations and events within one sport. Tennis, for example, consists of doubles and singles, while track and field contains many different events, from field events such as the javelin and shot put, to track events such as the 110-meter dash and the two-mile relay race.

Athletes train year-round, on their own or with a coach, friend, parent, or trainer. In addition to stretching and exercising the specific muscles used in any given sport, athletes concentrate on developing excellent eating and sleeping habits that will help them remain in top condition throughout the year. Although certain sports have a particular season, most professional athletes train rigorously all year, varying the type and duration of their workouts to develop strength, cardiovascular ability, flexibility, endurance, speed, and quickness, as well as to focus on technique and control. Often, an athlete's training focuses less on the overall game or program that the athlete will execute, than on specific areas or details of that game or program. Figure skaters, for example, won't simply keep going through their entire long programs from start to finish but instead will focus on the jumps, turns, and hand movements that refine the program. Similarly, sprinters don't keep running only the sprint distances they race in during a meet; instead, they vary their workouts to include some distance work, some sprints, a lot of weight training to build strength, and maybe some mental exercises to build control and focus while in the starter's blocks. Tennis players routinely spend hours just practicing their forehand, down-the-line shots.

Athletes often watch tapes or films of their previous practices or competitions to see where they can improve their performance. They also study what the other competitors are doing in order to prepare strategies for winning.

REQUIREMENTS

High School
A high school diploma will provide you with the basic skills that you will need in your long climb to becoming a professional athlete. Business and mathematics classes will teach you how to manage money wisely. Speech classes will help you become a better communicator. Physical education classes will help you build your strength, agility, and competitive spirit. You should, of course, participate in every organized sport that your school offers and that interests you.

Some individual sports such as tennis and gymnastics have professional competitors who are high school students. Teenagers in this situation often have private coaches with whom they practice both before and after going to school, and others are home-schooled as they travel to competitions.

Postsecondary Training
There are no formal education requirements for sports, although certain competitions and training opportunities are only available to those enrolled in four-year colleges and universities. Collegiate-level competitions are where most athletes in this area hone their skills; they may also compete in international or national competitions outside of college, but the chance to train and receive an education isn't one many serious athletes refuse. In fact, outstanding ability in athletics is the way many students pay for their college educations. Given the chances of striking it rich financially, an education (especially a free one) is a wise investment and one fully supported by most professional sports organizations.

Other Requirements
There is so much competition to be among the world's elite athletes in any given sport that talent alone isn't the primary requirement. Diligence, perseverance, hard work, ambition, and courage are all

Serena Williams positions herself for a forehand volley in the women's singles final against her sister, Venus Williams, during the U.S. Open. *(Susan Mullane, NewSport, Corbis)*

essential qualities to the individual who dreams of making a career as a professional athlete. "If you want to be a pro, there's no halfway. There's no three-quarters way," says Eric Roller, a former professional tennis player who competed primarily on the Florida circuit. Other, specific requirements will vary according to the sport. Jockeys, for example, are usually petite men and women.

EXPLORING

If you are interested in pursuing a career in professional sports, you should start participating in that sport as much and as early as possible. With some sports, an individual who is 15 years old may already be too old to realistically begin pursuing a professional career. By playing the sport and by talking to coaches, trainers, and athletes in the field, you can ascertain whether you like the sport enough to make it a career, determine if you have enough talent, and gain new insight into the field. You can also contact professional organizations and associations for information on how to best prepare for a career in their sport. Sometimes there are specialized training programs available, and the best way to find out is to get in contact with the people whose job it is to promote the sport.

EMPLOYERS

Professional athletes who compete in individual sports are not employed in the same manner as most workers. They do not work for employers, but choose the competitions or tournaments they wish to compete in. For example, a professional runner may choose to enter the Boston Marathon and then travel to Atlanta for the Peachtree Road Race.

STARTING OUT

Professional athletes must meet the requirements established by the organizing bodies of their respective sport. Sometimes this means meeting a physical requirement, such as age, height, or weight; and sometimes this means fulfilling a number of required stunts, or participating in a certain number of competitions. Professional organizations usually arrange it so that athletes can build up their skills and level of play by participating in lower-level competitions. College sports, as mentioned earlier, are an excellent way to improve one's skills while pursuing an education.

ADVANCEMENT

Professional athletes advance into the elite numbers of their sport by working and practicing hard, and by winning. Professional athletes usually obtain representation by sports agents in the behind-the-scenes deals that determine for which teams they will be playing and what they will be paid. These agents may also be involved with other key decisions involving commercial endorsements, personal income taxes, and financial investments of the athlete's revenues.

A college education can prepare all athletes for the day when their bodies can no longer compete at the top level, whether because of age or an unforeseen injury. Every athlete should be prepared to move into another career, related to the world of sports or not.

EARNINGS

The U.S. Department of Labor reports that athletes had median annual earnings of $41,060 in 2006. Ten percent earned less than $14,570 while the top 25 percent earned $94,040 or much more.

Salaries, prize monies, and commercial endorsements will vary from sport to sport; a lot depends on the popularity of the sport and its ability to attract spectators, or on the sport's professional organization and its ability to drum up sponsors for competitions and prize money. Still other sports, like boxing, depend on the skill of the fight's promoters to create interest in the fight. An elite professional tennis player who wins Wimbledon, for example, usually earns approximately $400,000 in a matter of several hours. Add to that the incredible sums a Wimbledon champion can make in endorsements and the tennis star can earn more than $1 million a year. This scenario is misleading, however. To begin with, top athletes usually cannot perform at such a level for very long, which is why a good accountant and investment counselor comes in handy. Secondly, for every top athlete who earns millions of dollars in a year, there are hundreds of professional athletes who earn less than $40,000. The stakes are incredibly high, the competition fierce.

Perhaps the only caveat to the financial success of an elite athlete is the individual's character or personality. An athlete with a bad temper or prone to unsportsmanlike behavior may still be able to set records or win games, but he or she won't necessarily be able to cash in on commercial endorsements. Advertisers are notoriously fickle about the spokespeople they choose to endorse products; some athletes have lost million-dollar accounts because of their bad behavior on and off the field of play.

Other options exist, thankfully, for professional athletes. Many go into some area of coaching, sports administration, management, or broadcasting. The professional athlete's unique insight and perspective can be a real asset in careers in these areas. Other athletes have been simultaneously pursuing other interests, some completely unrelated to their sport, such as education, business, social welfare, or the arts. Many continue to stay involved with the sport they have loved since childhood, coaching young children or volunteering with local school teams.

WORK ENVIRONMENT

Athletes compete in many different conditions, according to the setting of the sport (indoors or outdoors) and the rules of the organizing or governing bodies. Track-and-field athletes often compete in hot or rainy conditions, but at any point, organizing officials can call off the meet, or postpone competition until better weather. Indoor events are less subject to cancellation. However, since it is in the best interests of an organization not to risk the athletes' health, any condition that might adversely affect the outcome of a competition is usually reason enough to cancel or postpone it. An athlete, on the other hand, may withdraw from competition if he or she is injured or ill. Nerves and fear are not good reasons to default on a competition and part of ascending into the ranks of professional athletes means learning to cope with the anxiety that competition brings. Some athletes actually thrive on the nervous tension.

In order to reach the elite level of any sport, athletes must begin their careers early. Most professional athletes have been working at their sports since they were small children; skiers, figure skaters, and gymnasts, for example, begin skiing, skating, and tumbling as young as age two or three. Athletes have to fit hours of practice time into an already full day, usually several hours before school, and several hours after school. To make the situation more difficult, competitions and facilities for practice are often far from the young athlete's home, which means they either commute to and from practice and competitions with a parent, or they live with a coach or trainer for most of the year. Separation from a child's parents and family is an especially hard and frustrating element of the training program. When a child has demonstrated uncommon excellence in a sport, the family often decides to move to the city in which the sports facility is located, so that the child doesn't have to travel or be separated from a normal family environment.

The expenses of a sport can be overwhelming, as can the time an athlete must devote to practice and travel to and from competitions. In addition to specialized equipment and clothing, the athlete must pay for a coach, travel expenses, competition fees and, depending on the sport, time at the facility or gym where he or she practices. Tennis, golf, figure skating, and skiing are among the most expensive sports to enter.

Even with the years of hard work, practice, and financial sacrifice that most athletes and their families must endure, there is no guarantee that an athlete will achieve the rarest of the rare in the sports world—financial reward. An athlete needs to truly love the sport at which he or she excels, and also have a nearly insatiable ambition and work ethic.

OUTLOOK

The outlook for professional athletes will vary depending on the sport, its popularity, and the number of athletes currently competing. On the whole, the outlook for the field of professional sports is healthy, but the number of jobs will not increase dramatically. Some sports, however, may experience an increase in popularity, which will translate into greater opportunities for higher salaries, prize monies, and commercial endorsements.

FOR MORE INFORMATION

Individuals interested in becoming professional athletes should contact the professional organizations for the sport in which they would like to compete, such as the Professional Golfers' Association of America and the Professional Bowlers Association. Ask for information on requirements, training centers, and coaches. The following organization may also be able to provide further information:

American Alliance for Health, Physical Education, Recreation and Dance
1900 Association Drive
Reston, VA 20191-1598
Tel: 800-213-7193
http://www.aahperd.org

For a free brochure and information on the Junior Olympics and more, contact

Amateur Athletic Union
PO Box 22409
Lake Buena Vista, FL 32830-2409
Tel: 407-934-7200
http://www.aausports.org

Professional Athletes— Team Sports

OVERVIEW

Professional athletic teams compete against one another to win titles, championships, and series; team members are paid salaries and bonuses for their work. Team sports include football, basketball, hockey, baseball, and soccer.

HISTORY

The Olympic Games are generally credited as being the first instance of organized sports. Historians believe that they actually began as early as two centuries before the first written mention of them in 776 B.C. Rome's conquest of ancient Greece didn't bring the fabled games to a halt, but instead, the Romans added their own brand of sport to the list, including chariot-racing and gladiator battles. They built special arenas in which to stage these events, from the amphitheater to the renowned Colosseum in Rome. In A.D. 394, however, the Olympic Games were abolished and weren't revived until 1896.

In the interim, popular support for organized sports developed slowly. Tennis rose to popularity in France in the 1400s; historical records indicate that a track-and-field competition was held in England in 1510; Mary, Queen of Scots, loved to play golf and popularized the sport during her reign from 1542 to 1567; Her son, James I of England, lifted a ban on football (now known to Americans as soccer); and the first sweepstakes in horse racing was introduced in England in 1714.

The difference in the nature of sports before and after the 19th century largely has to do with organization. Prior to the 19th century, most sports were not officially organized; there were no official rules, competitions, or standards of play. During the 19th century, however, many sports underwent a transition from invented pastime to official sport. Rules governing play, the field of play, and competitions were agreed upon. The first modern track-and-field meet, for example, was held in England in 1825. Meanwhile, in the United States, the English game of rugby evolved into American football. The first game was played between Rutgers and Princeton in 1869.

Team sports, in contrast with individual sports, take advantage of the fact that more than one person is allowed to play by assigning different roles to different players. Each team member usually has a specific task, one at which he or she excels.

Baseball, basketball, golf, tennis, and then boxing began to attract large crowds of people in the early 20th century. As these sports and others grew in popularity, governing bodies and organizations were created to oversee the fair play of each sport. Gradually, coverage of sporting events on radio and in newspapers began to grow until sports quite literally became the national pastime for Americans. Sports stars became as renowned as movie stars or politicians, sometimes even more so.

Today, the number of professional team sports is growing, but the numbers still favor male athletes. Only a few professional teams exist for female athletes, none of which are currently promoted or supported by the media and public to the degree that are male teams. The performance of women athletes in the 1996 Olympic Games held in Atlanta, Georgia, such as the women's softball team, and the creation of a women's professional basketball league, the Women's National Basketball Association (WNBA) in the late-1990s, may indicate the tide is turning.

THE JOB

Unlike amateur athletes who play or compete in amateur circles for titles or trophies only, professional athletic teams compete against one another to win titles, championships, and series; team members are paid salaries and bonuses for their work.

The athletic performances of individual teams are evaluated according to the nature and rules of each specific sport: Usually the winning team compiles the highest score, as in football, basketball, and soccer. Competitions are organized by local, regional, national, and international organizations and associations whose primary functions are to promote the sport and sponsor competitive events.

Within a professional sport there are usually different levels of competition based on age, ability, and gender. There are often different designations and divisions within one sport. Professional baseball, for example, is made up of the two major leagues (American and National) each made up of three divisions, East, Central, and West; and the minor leagues (single-A, double-A, triple-A). All of these teams are considered professional because the players are compensated for their work, but the financial rewards are the greatest in the major leagues.

Whatever the team sport, most team members specialize in a specific area of the game. In gymnastics, for example, the entire six-member team trains on all of the gymnastic apparatuses—balance beam, uneven bars, vault, and floor exercise—but usually each of the six gymnasts excels in only one or two areas. Those gymnasts who do excel in all four events are likely to do well in the individual, all-around title, which is a part of the team competition. Team members in football, basketball, baseball, soccer, and hockey all assume different positions, some of which change depending on whether or not the team is trying to score a goal (offensive positions) or prevent the opposition from scoring one (defensive positions). During team practices, athletes focus on their specific role in a game, whether that is defensive, offensive, or both. For example, a pitcher will spend some time running bases and throwing to other positions, but the majority of his or her time will most likely be spent practicing pitching.

Professional teams train for most of the year, but unlike athletes in individual sports, athletes who are members of a team usually have more of an off-season. The training programs of professional athletes differ according to the season. Following an off-season, most team sports have a training season, in which they begin to focus their workouts after a period of relative inactivity to develop or maintain strength, cardiovascular ability, flexibility, endurance, speed, and quickness, as well as to focus on technique and control. During the season, the team coach, physician, trainers, and physical therapists organize specific routines, programs, or exercises to target game skills as well as individual athletic weaknesses, whether skill-related or from injury.

These workouts also vary according to the difficulty of the game schedule. During a playoff or championship series, the coach and athletic staff realize that a rigorous workout in between games might tax the athletes' strength, stamina, or even mental preparedness, jeopardizing the outcome of the next game. Instead, the coach might prescribe a mild workout followed by intensive stretching. In addition to stretching and exercising the specific muscles used in any given sport, athletes concentrate on developing excellent eating and sleeping habits that will help them remain in top condition throughout the year. Abstaining from drinking alcoholic beverages during a season is a practice to which many professional athletes adhere.

The coaching or training staff often films the games and practices so that the team can benefit from watching their individual exploits, as well as their combined play. By watching their performances, team members can learn how to improve their techniques and strategies. It is common for professional teams to also study other teams' moves and strategies in order to determine a method of coping with the other teams' plays during a game.

REQUIREMENTS

High School

Most professional athletes demonstrate tremendous skill and interest in their sport well before high school. High school offers student athletes the opportunity to gain experience in the field in a structured and competitive environment. Under the guidance of a coach, you can begin developing suitable training programs for yourself and learn about health, nutrition, and conditioning issues.

High school also offers you the opportunity to experiment with a variety of sports and a variety of positions within a sport. Most junior varsity and some varsity high school teams allow you to try out different positions and begin to discover whether you have more of an aptitude for the defensive dives of a goalie or for the forwards' front-line action. High school coaches will help you learn to expand upon your strengths and abilities and develop yourself more fully as an athlete. High school is also an excellent time to begin developing the concentration powers, leadership skills, and good sportsmanship necessary for success in the field.

People who hope to become professional athletes should take a full load of high school courses including four years of English, math, and science as well as health and physical education. A solid high school education will help ensure success in college (often the next step in becoming a professional athlete) and may help you in earning a college athletic scholarship. A high school diploma will certainly give you something to fall back on if an injury, a change in career goals, or other circumstance prevents you from earning a living as an athlete.

Postsecondary Training

College is important for future professional athletes for several reasons. It provides the opportunity to gain skill and strength in your

Green Bay Packers quarterback Brett Favre prepares to throw to a receiver during a game against the Minnesota Vikings. *(Layne Kennedy, Corbis)*

sport before you try to succeed in the pros, and it also offers you the chance of being observed by professional scouts.

Perhaps most importantly, however, a college education arms you with a valuable degree that you can use if you do not earn a living as a professional athlete or after your performance career ends. College athletes major in everything from communications to pre-med and enjoy careers as coaches, broadcasters, teachers, doctors, actors, and business people, to name a few. As with high school sports, college athletes must maintain certain academic standards in order to be permitted to compete in intercollegiate play.

Other Requirements

If you want to be a professional athlete, you must be fully committed to succeeding. You must work almost nonstop to improve your conditioning and skills and not give up when you don't succeed as quickly or as easily as you had hoped. And even then, because the competition is so fierce, the goal of earning a living as a professional athlete is still difficult to reach. For this reason, professional athletes must not get discouraged easily. They must have the self-confidence and ambition to keep working and keep trying. Professional athletes must also have a love for their sport that compels them to want to reach their fullest potential.

EXPLORING

Students interested in pursuing a career in professional sports should start playing that sport as much and as early as possible. Most junior high and high schools have well-established programs in the sports that have professional teams.

If a team sport does not exist in your school, that does not mean your chances at playing it have evaporated. Petition your school board to establish it as a school sport and set aside funds for it. In the meantime, organize other students into a club team, scheduling practices and unofficial games. If the sport is a recognized team sport in the United States or Canada, contact the professional organization for the sport for additional information; if anyone would have helpful tips for gaining recognition, the professional organization would. Also, try calling the local or state athletic board to see what other schools in your area recognizes it as a team sport. Then make a list of those teams and try scheduling exhibition games with them. Your goal is to show that other students have a definite interest in the game and that other schools recognize it.

To determine if you really want to commit to pursuing a professional career in your team sport, talk to coaches, trainers, and any athletes who are currently pursuing a professional career. You can also contact professional organizations and associations for information on how to best prepare for a career in their sport. Sometimes there are specialized training programs available, and the best way to find out is to get in contact with the people whose job it is to promote the sport.

EMPLOYERS

Professional athletes are employed by private and public ownership groups throughout the United States and Canada. At the highest male professional level, there are 32 National Football League franchises, 30 Major League Baseball franchises, 30 National Basketball Association franchises, 30 National Hockey League franchises, and 13 Major League Soccer franchises. The Women's National Basketball Association has 13 franchises.

STARTING OUT

Most team sports have some official manner of establishing which teams acquire which players; often, this is referred to as a draft, although sometimes members of a professional team are chosen through a competition. Usually, the draft occurs between the college and professional levels of the sport. The National Basketball Association (NBA), for example, has its NBA College Draft. During the draft, the owners and managers of professional basketball teams choose players in an order based on the team's performance in the previous season. This means that the team with the worst record in the previous season has a greater chance of getting to choose first from the list of available players.

Furthermore, professional athletes must meet the requirements established by the organizing bodies of their respective sport. Sometimes this means meeting a physical requirement, such as age, height, and weight; and sometimes this means fulfilling a number of required stunts, or participating in a certain number of competitions. Professional organizations usually arrange it so that athletes can build up their skills and level of play by participating in lower-level competitions. College sports, as mentioned before, are an excellent way to improve one's skills while pursuing an education.

ADVANCEMENT

Professional athletes in team sports advance in three ways: when their team advances, when they are traded to better teams, and when they negotiate better contracts. In all three instances, this is achieved by the individual team member who works and practices hard, and who gives his or her best performance in game after game. Winning teams also receive a deluge of media attention that often creates celebrities out of individual players, which in turn provides these top players with opportunities for financially rewarding commercial endorsements.

Professional athletes are usually represented by sports agents in the behind-the-scenes deals that determine for which teams they will be playing and what they will be paid. These agents may also be involved with other key decisions involving commercial endorsements, personal income taxes, and financial investments of the athlete's revenues.

In the moves from high school athletics to collegiate athletics and from collegiate athletics to the pros, coaches and scouts are continually scouring the ranks of high school and college teams for new talent; they are most interested in the athletes who consistently deliver points or prevent the opposition from scoring. There is simply no substitute for success.

A college education, however, can prepare all athletes for the day when their bodies can no longer compete at the top level, whether because of age or an unforeseen injury. Every athlete should be prepared to move into another career, related to the world of sports or not.

Professional athletes do have other options, especially those who have graduated from a four-year college or university. Many go into some area of coaching, sports administration, management, or broadcasting. The professional athlete's unique insight and perspective can be a real asset in these careers. Other athletes simultaneously pursue other interests, some completely unrelated to their sport, such as education, business, social welfare, or the arts. Many continue to stay involved with the sport they have loved since childhood, coaching young children or volunteering with local school teams.

EARNINGS

In 2006, athletes had median annual earnings of $41,060, according to the U.S. Department of Labor. Ten percent earned less than $14,570 while the highest paid 25 percent earned $94,040 or much more. Perhaps the only caveat to the financial success of an elite athlete is the individual's character or personality. An athlete with a bad temper or prone to unsportsmanlike behavior may still be able to participate in team play, helping to win games and garner trophies, but he or she will not necessarily be able to cash in on the commercial endorsements. Advertisers are notoriously fickle about the spokespeople they choose to endorse products; some athletes have lost million-dollar accounts because of their bad behavior on and off the court.

WORK ENVIRONMENT

Athletes compete in many different conditions, according to the setting of the sport (indoors or outdoors) and the rules of the organizing or governing bodies. Athletes who participate in football or soccer, for example, often compete in hot, rainy, or freezing conditions, but at any point, organizing officials can call off the match, or postpone competition until better weather.

Indoor events are less subject to cancellation. However, since it is in the best interests of an organization not to risk the athletes' health, any condition that might adversely affect the outcome of a competition is usually reason to cancel or postpone it. The coach or team physician, on the other hand, may withdraw an athlete from a game if he or she is injured or ill. Nerves and fear are not good reasons to default on a competition, and part of ascending into the ranks of professional athletes means learning to cope with the anxiety that comes with competition. Some athletes, however, actually thrive on the nervous tension.

In order to reach the elite level of any sport, athletes must begin their careers early. Most professional athletes have been honing their skills since they were quite young. Athletes fit hours of practice time into an already full day; many famous players practiced on their own in the hours before school, as well as for several hours after school during team practice. Competitions are often far from the young athlete's home, which means they must travel on a bus or in a van with the team and coaching staff. Sometimes young athletes are placed in special training programs far from their homes and parents. They live with other athletes training for the same sport or on the same team and only see their parents for holidays and vacations. The separation from a child's parents and family can be difficult; often an athlete's family decides to move to be closer to the child's training facility.

The expenses of a sport can be overwhelming, as is the time an athlete must devote to practice and travel to and from competitions. Although most high school athletic programs pay for many expenses, if the athlete wants additional training or private coaching, the child's parents must come up with the extra money. Sometimes, young athletes can get official sponsors or they might qualify for an athletic scholarship from the training program. In addition to specialized equipment and clothing, the athlete must sometimes pay for a coach, travel expenses, competition fees and, depending on the sport, time at the facility or gym where he or she practices. Gymnasts, for example, train for years as individuals, and then compete for positions on national or international teams. Up until the time they are accepted (and usually during their participation in the team), these gymnasts must pay for their expenses—from coach to travel to uniforms to room and board away from home.

Even with the years of hard work, practice, and financial sacrifice that most athletes and their families must endure, there is no guarantee that an athlete will achieve the rarest of the rare in the sports world—financial reward. An athlete needs to truly love the sport at which he or she excels and also have a nearly insatiable ambition and work ethic.

OUTLOOK

The outlook for professional athletes will vary depending on the sport, its popularity, and the number of positions open with professional teams. On the whole, the outlook for the field of professional sports is healthy, but the number of jobs will not increase dramatically. Some sports, however, may experience a rise in popularity, which will translate into greater opportunities for higher salaries, prize monies, and commercial endorsements.

FOR MORE INFORMATION

Individuals interested in pursuing a career in a professional team sport should speak to their coach and contact the professional organization for that sport to receive further information. For other ideas on how to pursue a career in a professional team sport, contact

American Alliance for Health, Physical Education, Recreation and Dance
1900 Association Drive
Reston, VA 20191-1598
Tel: 800-213-7193
http://www.aahperd.org

For a free brochure and information on the Junior Olympics and more, contact

Amateur Athletic Union
PO Box 22409
Lake Buena Vista, FL 32830-2409
Tel: 407-934-7200
http://www.aausports.org

Sporting Goods Production Workers

QUICK FACTS

School Subjects
Physical education
Technical/shop

Personal Skills
Following instructions
Mechanical/manipulative

Work Environment
Primarily indoors
Primarily one location

Minimum Education Level
High school diploma

Salary Range
$12,168 to $20,800 to
$45,760

Certification or Licensing
None available

Outlook
More slowly than the average

DOT
732

GOE
08.03.01, 08.03.06

NOC
9619

O*NET-SOC
51-4011.01, 51-2092.00,
51-6051.00, 51-9061.00

OVERVIEW

Sporting goods production workers manufacture, assemble, and finish sporting goods equipment such as golf clubs, fishing tackle, basketballs, footballs, skis, and baseball equipment. Their tasks range from operating machines to fine handcrafting of equipment.

HISTORY

Throughout history, every society and culture has developed games and sports for relaxation and competition. Bowling, for example, has been around for centuries; a stone ball and nine stone pins were found in the ancient tomb of an Egyptian child. Polo is believed to have originated in Asia and was brought back to England and America by British officers returning from India in the 1800s. Native American peoples played lacrosse with webbed sticks and hard wooden balls centuries ago. Soccer, arguably the world's most popular sport, was invented in England, where a version of the game was played nearly 2,000 years ago.

Some of the most popular sports in America have a relatively recent history. Basketball was invented in 1891 by Dr. James Naismith in Springfield, Massachusetts; its popularity grew so quickly that it became an Olympic event in 1936. Ice hockey as we know it was invented in Canada in the 1870s. It quickly became popular in northern countries and was inaugurated as an Olympic sport in 1920. In the 1870s football started as a college sport that mixed elements of soccer and rugby and soon developed its own set of rules. Although folklore attributes the invention of baseball to Abner Doubleday in 1839, people were playing it for many years before then.

Some games, both ancient and modern, have changed little since the time they were first played. Soccer, for instance, has remained popular in part because of its simplicity; the only equipment needed to play is a ball. Other sports have grown to require more elaborate equipment. Modern technology has been applied to many aspects of sport and given us such improvements as better protective padding, livelier tennis rackets, and stronger golf balls. Computers are used to improve the design and composition of sports gear. The equipment used in each sport is unique in design and manufacture and is put together by skilled specialists.

THE JOB

Every sport involves its own equipment, and each kind of equipment is made somewhat differently. Basketballs and volleyballs are made by approximately the same process, which differs from the processes for making footballs and baseballs. But the manufacturing processes for sporting goods and for other products are also similar in many ways.

As in the manufacturing of other products, *machine operators* control large machine tools, such as presses, and smaller tools, such as saws and sewing machines. After they have done their tasks, they may pass the work on to different kinds of assemblers. *Floor assemblers* operate large machines and power tools; *bench assemblers* work with smaller machines to complete a product and perhaps to test it; *precision assemblers* perform highly skilled assembly work. They may work closely with engineers and technicians to develop and test new products and designs. These general categories can be applied to many of the occupations involved in sporting goods manufacturing, although the job titles vary with different kinds of products.

In the manufacturing of golf equipment, for example, the shaft of a golf club and the head, or club end, are made separately and are then assembled, weighted, and balanced. *Golf-club assemblers* do much of the work. They use bench-mounted circular saws to cut the shaft for a club to a specified length, depending on the model of club being made. *Golf-club head formers* hammer precast metal club heads to the correct angle and then glue the proper club head onto a shaft and secure the head by drilling a small hole and inserting a pin. Wooden clubs are glued together the same way, except that once the assembly has dried, the weight of the club is checked and adjusted for the model type. *Assemblers* or *golf-club weighters* can adjust the weight by drilling a hole into the head and adding molten lead or threaded cylindrical metal weights.

Grip wrappers attach the handle of the golf club. They insert a club in a rotating machine, brush adhesive on the shaft, attach a leather strap, and then carefully spin the shaft to cover it tightly and evenly with the leather strap. When they are finished, they trim the excess leather and fasten the grip in place with tape or a sleeve. Finally, *golf-club head inspectors* examine the head to verify that it conforms to specifications.

The manufacturing of fishing equipment is another instance of a production process involving a series of workers. It begins with *fishing-rod markers,* who mark the places on rod blanks where the line guides and decorative markings should be put. After this, *fishing-rod assemblers* use liquid cement to attach the hardware, such as reel seats, handles, and line guides, onto the rods. Line guides can also be attached with thread by *guide winders*, who decorate the rods by winding thread around them at intervals. Finally, *fishing-reel assemblers* assemble the parts of the intricate reel mechanisms, test the reels, and then attach them to rods.

Some processes used in manufacturing sporting goods, such as lathing (which is used in making baseball bats) and vulcanizing (which is used in making hockey pucks), are commonly used in making many other products as well. But other processes are more specialized. To make basketballs, volleyballs, and soccer balls, for example, *ball assemblers* cement panels of rubberized fabric onto a hollow, spherical frame made of wax. A door opening is left in the ball carcass so that the wax frame can be broken and removed piece by piece. Once this is done, a bladder is inserted into the ball and inflated to a specific pressure. The flaps of the door opening are then aligned with the other seams of the ball and cemented onto the bladder, and the ball is complete.

Some baseball equipment is still made by hand, much the same way it was many years ago. Many wooden bats are hand-turned to the specifications of each player. Danny Luckett makes Louisville Slugger bats in Louisville, Kentucky, and has personally finished bats for many major league players. "We used to do everything by hand, but now a tracing machine helps make the bats," says Luckett, who has worked for 30 years for the Hillerich & Bradsby Company, which is the manufacturer of Louisville Slugger bats. "The machine is similar to a key-making machine and uses a template. Before, we could make 32 to 35 in a day, and now we can make 250 to 260 in a day."

Baseballs themselves are assembled by *hand baseball sewers*, who cement the leather hide of the ball to the core and sew the sections of hide together using a harness needle and waxed linen thread. To make baseball gloves, *lacers* sew precut pieces of leather together, working with the glove inside out. Then *lining inserters* put a lining in place, and *reversers* turn the glove right-side out on a series of posts. Next, *baseball glove shapers* use a heated, hand-shaped form to open and stretch the finger linings. With various rubber mallets, they hammer the seams smooth and form the glove pocket. Finally, they try on the glove and pound the pocket to make sure that it fits comfortably.

As these examples show, the manufacturing of sporting goods involves ordinary industrial processes that are adapted to suit each product. Within the limits of sports safety and economical operation of their plants, sporting goods manufacturers are constantly trying to improve designs and manufacturing processes to make equipment that is reliable and durable and maximizes athletic performance.

REQUIREMENTS

While most employers prefer that employees have a high school diploma, it is not a requirement for many jobs in this industry. Employers look for workers who can do accurate, high-quality work at a fast pace. Most employees in the industry learn their skills through on-the-job training. Training may take from a few days to several months, depending on the job.

High School

High school courses that can help prepare students for working in the sporting goods equipment industry include shop, basic mathematics, blueprint reading, sewing, and other classes that provide practice in following written instructions and diagrams or making items by hand. Speech classes will also be helpful. "It's important to be have good communication skills," says Danny Luckett. "You have to pay attention to details."

Postsecondary Training

Electronic devices are used more and more in sports for purposes such as timing skiers and runners. As more applications are developed for electronic and electrical equipment, more manufacturing workers will be needed who have the kind of knowledge and training

The Most Popular Sports and Exercise Activities, 2006

The National Sporting Goods Association asked Americans age seven and older what sports and exercise activities they participated in more than once in 2006. The most popular activities were:

1. Exercise/Walking: 87.5 million
2. Swimming: 56.5 million
3. Exercising with Equipment: 52.4 million
4. Bowling: 44.8 million
5. Workout at Fitness Center: 36.9 million
6. Bicycle Riding: 35.6 million
7. Aerobic Exercise: 33.7 million
8. Weightlifting: 32.9 million
9. Hiking: 31.0 million
10. Running/Jogging: 28.8 million

that is available at technical schools. Also, design, precision assembly, and production jobs increasingly rely on machinery that is controlled by computers. For these reasons, a background that includes training in electronics and computer applications is very important for many jobs in this industry.

Other Requirements

Sports equipment production workers generally need good eyesight and manual dexterity to work with small parts and operate machines. Interest in sports can be an advantage. For example, it helps for workers who shape baseball gloves to have experience playing baseball and using gloves, so they know the feel of a good fit.

"I used to play [baseball] when I was younger," says Luckett. "It's kind of neat now to watch the games and know that we have a part in it."

Some sporting goods production workers belong to labor unions. Luckett belongs to the United Steelworkers of America. Another union is UNITE HERE, which represents workers who make shoes, caps, hats, uniforms, ski suits, golf gloves, leotards, and other apparel. Other unions include the United Food and Commercial Workers International Union; the International Textile, Garment and Leather Workers' Federation; the Laborers' International Union of North

America; the International Brotherhood of Electrical Workers; and the International Brotherhood of Boilermakers, Iron Ship Builders, Blacksmiths, Forgers, and Helpers.

EXPLORING

To learn something about what the work is like in the sporting goods production business, you can try to get a summer job working in a nearby sports equipment factory. Such a job is likely to be in a warehouse or in custodial services, but it may still offer you a chance to observe the manufacturing processes firsthand and to talk with experienced employees about their jobs. Working part time can also be an opportunity to show an employer that you are dependable and have good work habits, and it could lead to permanent employment in the future. Since an interest in sports is helpful, knowledge of sports and sports equipment gained through actual participation would be beneficial.

EMPLOYERS

There are more than 3,000 manufacturers of sporting goods equipment in the United States, according the Sporting Goods Manufacturers Association (SGMA). They are located throughout the United States and may be small companies or large conglomerates. The recent trend toward mergers has affected this industry; fewer companies are employing more workers.

STARTING OUT

Job seekers in this field can contact sporting goods manufacturers directly to learn whether or not they have any job openings. Other possibilities for job leads include checking the listings at the local offices of the state employment service and in the classified sections of newspapers. School counselors can provide information about local companies that are looking for workers.

ADVANCEMENT

Newly hired employees in sporting goods factories usually are assigned simple tasks. Trainees may acquire their job skills informally as they work beside and watch more experienced workers. Others may enter into a formal training program. Workers who have completed training for their job category and have shown they can meet production requirements may be able move into higher paying production jobs as they become available.

"Here, you're not really hired to do one specific job, but jobs are filled from within and you start where there is an opening," says Danny Luckett about the baseball bat manufacturer for which he works.

In companies that are large and diversified, workers may advance to jobs in other divisions. Qualified employees may also move to positions as product inspectors or supervisors of other production workers. Moving into management jobs usually requires further experience, technical training, and formal education in business subjects.

Some knowledgeable, experienced people with new product ideas or an urge for independence may decide to start their own sporting goods production company. Setting up a new business in any field is a risky venture, however, and anyone who is interested in taking this step needs first to take a hard and informed look at the high costs involved, in addition to the potential benefits.

EARNINGS

According to the U.S. Department of Labor, the median hourly earnings of machine setters, operators and tenders employed in all industries ranged from about $8 to $22 in 2006 (or $16,640 to $45,760 annually for full-time work). Assemblers had earnings than ranged from less than $8 an hour to $18 or more per hour in 2006. Beginning workers often start at between minimum wage and $8.50 per hour ($12,168 to $17,680 annually for full-time work). Wages are generally higher for skilled, experienced machine operators. Most workers also get fringe benefits, such as health insurance, paid holidays and vacation days, and pension plans. Some firms offer stock options to employees.

WORK ENVIRONMENT

Conditions in plants vary, with some factories having modern, well-equipped, well-lit work stations for employees. Other plants provide less comfortable working conditions. In some jobs, employees have to sit or stand in one place for the entire work shift, while other jobs require heavy lifting, hammering, or other physically strenuous activities. People who operate presses, molds, and other heavy machinery may have to load and remove heavy work pieces made of leather, metal, fiberglass, plastic, and other materials. Almost all workers have production quotas to meet, which can be stressful at times.

Heat, noise, dust, or strong odors are unavoidable in many production jobs. Workers may need to wear safety glasses, hard hats, earplugs, or other protective clothing.

Sports equipment production workers average 40 hours of work per week. Many factories operate two or three shifts a day, so employees may be required to work days, evenings, nights, or weekends.

OUTLOOK

As sports and fitness become more popular among health-conscious Americans, the market for sporting goods is expected to continue to grow. Exports of American-made goods may also increase in coming years.

This does not mean, however, that the number of jobs in sporting goods manufacturing will also increase. The manufacture of many kinds of sports gear is very labor-intensive, and to keep labor costs down, manufacturers have moved some of their operations to plants in other countries, where workers can be paid lower wages. In addition, advances in automation, robotics, and computer-aided manufacturing are allowing companies to phase out certain production jobs. In the future, the need will be for employees who can program machines, supervise production, and manage resources. Workers will also be needed to test product safety and quality.

The sporting goods manufacturing industry is generally a solid but not expanding business. Job turnover is fairly high among production and assembly workers, so most new workers will be hired to replace people who leave their jobs.

FOR MORE INFORMATION

For industry information and job listings, contact
Sporting Goods Manufacturers Association
1150 17th Street, NW
Washington, DC 20036-4603
Tel: 202-775-1762
Email: info@sgma.com
http://sgma.com

Sport Psychologists

QUICK FACTS

School Subjects
Biology
Health
Psychology

Personal Skills
Communication/ideas
Helping/teaching

Work Environment
Primarily indoors
Primarily one location

Minimum Education Level
Master's degree

Salary Range
$35,280 to $59,440 to
$102,730+

Certification or Licensing
Required by all states

Outlook
Little or no change

DOT
045

GOE
12.02.02

NOC
4151

O*NET-SOC
19-3031.00, 19-3031.01,
19-3031.02

OVERVIEW

In general, *sport psychologists* work with amateur and professional athletes to improve their mental and physical health, as well as athletic performances, by using goal setting, imagery, focus strategies, and relaxation techniques, among others. Sport psychologists also strive to help athletes to mentally prepare for competition. There are approximately 179,000 psychologists employed in the United States, although sport psychologists comprise only a small segment of this number.

HISTORY

In the 17th century, French philosopher René Descartes described his belief that human behaviors could be classified in two ways—voluntary and involuntary. Behaviors that were completely mechanical, instinctual, and similar to those of animals, he characterized as involuntary; behaviors that required or submitted to reason were characterized as voluntary. Based on this early model, and the subsequent work of others, including John Locke, James Mill, and John Stuart Mill, later philosophers and scientists experimented with sensation and perception, culminating with an introspective analysis of the many elements of an individual's experience.

William James advanced modern psychology by asserting the theory of a stream of thought; G. Stanley Hall, a contemporary of James, established the first true laboratory of psychology at Clark University in 1883. Sigmund Freud introduced the medical tradition to clinical psychology. A physician and neurologist, Freud's methods of psychoanalysis included word association techniques and later, inkblot techniques as developed by Hermann Rorschach.

After World War II, psychology became formally recognized as a profession. The American Psychological Association has developed standards of training for psychologists, and certification and licensing laws have been passed to regulate the practice of professional psychology.

Since psychology deals with human behavior, psychologists apply their knowledge and techniques to a wide range of endeavors including human services, management, law, and sports.

THE JOB

Sport and exercise psychology is the scientific study of the psychological factors that are associated with participation and performance in sport, exercise, and other types of physical activity. In general, sport psychologists work with amateur and professional athletes to improve their mental and physical health, as well as athletic performances, by using goal setting, imagery, focus strategies, and relaxation techniques, among others. Sport psychologists also strive to help athletes to mentally prepare for competition.

Sport psychologists are divided into three categories: clinical, educational, and research. *Clinical sport psychologists* work mainly with individuals who are experiencing emotional problems that are usually, but not always, somehow connected to their sport. *Educational sport psychologists* have two roles, one as a classroom instructor and the other as a consultant. In the classroom, they teach students methods and techniques related to sport psychology. On the field, they usually function as members of the coaching staff. Just as the coach teaches physical skills, the sport psychologist teaches mental skills. *Research sport psychologists* conduct studies that provide the clinical and educational sport psychologists with scientific facts and statistics.

All sport psychology professionals are interested in two main objectives: helping athletes use psychological principles to improve performance (performance enhancement) and understanding how participation in sport, exercise, and physical activity affects an individual's psychological development, health, and well-being throughout the life span.

Sport psychologists work with individual athletes and entire teams. They may concentrate on the problems the athlete is having with the sport, from a bad slump to the feelings of low self-esteem that come when the crowd jeers the athlete's performance. Sport psychologists also work to help the individual athlete to overcome feelings of depression, drug or substance abuse, and violence.

They work with teams in many ways, the most notable of which is creating a feeling of cohesion among the many different personalities that constitute a team. Team members are also counseled when they are traded to another team or released.

Sport psychologists also work with individual athletes and team members on improving their level of performance, concentration, and mental attitude. The phrase "a winning attitude" derives its power from the fact that sport psychologists can help the athletes with whom they work to actually visualize a winning shot or a perfect golf swing and then execute that vision.

Sport psychologists don't work with only elite athletes or teams; most sport psychologists, in fact, work with college athletes or amateur athletes, and many teach in academic settings or offer motivational lecture series. Some sport psychologists have their own columns in specialized sports magazines and others work in athletic training facilities, hired full time by the owners to work with the athletes who come there to train.

Sport psychology consultants provide many of the same services as sport psychologists but do not treat psychopathology (depression, eating disorders, drug addiction, etc.) since only licensed therapists and sport psychologists are qualified to do so. "A sport psychology consultant works on mental skills training with teams and individual athletes," says Carrie Cheadle, a sport psychology consultant in private practice in northern California. "They help athletes work towards improving their physical performance by addressing the mental attributes necessary to be successful in sport. They address topics such as goal setting, relaxation, motivation, group dynamics, focus, etc. Many also address life skills (stress management, leadership, time management, etc.) as well." According to the AASP, sport psychology consultants typically work with a variety of individuals involved in sport and exercise, including athletes at all levels, athletes with disabilities, recreational athletes, injured athletes, exercise participants, group exercise leaders and personal trainers, health club instructors and administrators, coaches and administrators at all levels, and athletic trainers. Sport psychology consultants are also known as *mental skills coaches* and *performance enhancement consultants*.

REQUIREMENTS

The requirements for entering the field of sports medicine as a sport psychologist are somewhat tricky to understand, so it helps to understand the various paths available in psychology in general, as determined by the American Psychological Association. Students should expect to spend five to seven years in graduate work for a doctoral degree.

High School
High school students should take a college preparatory curriculum that concentrates on English, mathematics, and sciences. You should also take a foreign language, especially French and German, because reading comprehension of these languages is one of the usual requirements for obtaining a doctoral degree. Participation in sports will give you the background necessary to effectively understand the athletes you work with in your practice.

Postsecondary Training
A doctoral degree is generally required for employment as a psychologist, but there are two different degrees that psychologists can seek at the doctorate level. The first degree is called the Ph.D., and psychologists with this degree qualify for a wide range of teaching, research, clinical, and counseling positions in universities, elementary and secondary schools, and private industry. The second degree is called a Psy.D. (doctor of psychology); psychologists with this degree qualify mainly for clinical positions. The Ph.D. degree culminates in a dissertation based on original research, while the Psy.D. is usually based on practical work and examinations rather than a dissertation. In clinical or counseling psychology, the requirements for a doctoral degree usually include a year or more of internship or supervised experience.

Individuals who have only a master's degree in psychology are allowed to administer tests as psychological assistants and, if they are under the supervision of doctoral-level psychologists, they can conduct research in laboratories, conduct psychological evaluations, counsel patients, and perform administrative duties. They are also allowed to teach in high schools and two-year colleges and work as school psychologists or counselors.

Those individuals with only a bachelor's degree in psychology can assist psychologists and other professionals and work as research or administrative assistants, but without further academic training they cannot advance further in psychology.

Having said all of this, it will perhaps come as a shock that there are no sport psychology doctoral programs accredited by the American Psychological Association (APA). One of the controversies behind this is whether professionals working with athletes in applied areas of sport psychology should be required to have doctoral training in clinical or counseling psychology—training which would qualify them to provide psychological treatment to athletes as well. The solution reached by the APA, along with the Association for the Advancement of Applied Sports Psychology (AAASP) and the North American Society for the Psychology of Sport and Physical Activity, is that any practitioners of sport psychology who do not also have doctoral-level clinical or counseling training should refer athletes who need treatment to licensed professionals. Sport psychologists who work with Olympic athletes are required to have doctoral-level degrees.

Those students who are interested in academic teaching and research in sport psychology can earn doctoral degrees in sport sciences and take additional courses in psychology or counseling. Over 50 schools in the United States offer this type of program, including the University of North Carolina–Greensboro (http://www.uncg.edu) and the University of Florida (http://www.ufl.edu). Typical subjects covered include sport psychology, performance enhancement, concentration skills, stress and attention management, and motivation.

Those students who want more emphasis on psychology in their training can pursue a psychology doctorate in areas such as group procedures, psychotherapy, learning, education, and human development or motivation, with a subspecialty in sport psychology. At most universities, students take courses like these in the sport sciences department, while at a few schools, such as the University of Washington (http://www.washington.edu) and the University of California–Los Angeles (http://www.ucla.edu), it is possible to take similar courses through the psychology department.

Students who wish to provide clinical services to athletes can pursue a doctoral degree in APA-accredited clinical or counseling psychology programs, with a concentration in sport psychology. This track offers students the widest range of job opportunities, from teaching and research in sports and psychology to counseling athletes as well as the general population. An institution where this mode of study is typical is the University of North Texas (http://www.unt.edu).

For those students who are interested primarily in educating people about the health benefits of exercise or in helping student athletes, a master's degree is an option. More than 100 sport sciences departments offer a master's degree in areas related to sport psychology.

For more detailed information on graduate programs in psychology and sport psychology, look for *The Directory of Graduate Programs in Applied Sport Psychology*, edited by Michael L. Sachs, Kevin L. Burke, and Diana C. Schrader (Morgantown, W.Va.: Fitness Information Technology, 2006).

Certification or Licensing

The AASP offers the certified consultant designation to members who meet educational requirements and accrue a specified numbers of hours of supervised experience in sport and exercise psychology.

Most states require that all practitioners of psychology meet licensing requirements if they are in independent practice or involved in offering patient care of any kind (including clinical and counseling). Once the educational requirements are fulfilled, a sport psychologist should contact the AAASP for details about licensing requirements, as they usually vary from state to state.

Other Requirements

Because sport psychology is such a broad field, various personal attributes apply to different psychology positions. Clinical sport psychologists should be able to relate to others and have excellent listening skills. Educational sport psychologists should have strong communication skills in order to convey ideas and concepts to students and clients. Research sport psychologists should be analytical and detail oriented and have strong writing and mathematics skills.

EXPLORING

You can gain experience in this field by volunteering to work for research programs at area universities or by working in the office of a psychologist. Another option is to learn more about sports by working as a gofer or intern with the sports medicine departments of college, university, or professional athletic teams. Even by participating in a sport in high school or college, you can gain valuable insight into the mental and emotional stresses and demands placed upon athletes.

In addition, students should begin their understanding of psychology by taking as many courses in the field as possible.

EMPLOYERS

Sport psychologists are employed by athletes at the amateur, college, or professional level and by owners of professional, college, and private organizations. They may also be employed at colleges and universities as teachers and researchers.

STARTING OUT

Along the road toward a Ph.D. or Psy.D., students of all levels can get involved in the research or educational aspects of psychology, either as a volunteer subject or a paid helper. These positions will gradually increase in responsibility and scope as the student progresses in his or her studies. Eventually, the student will be eligible for internships that will, in turn, provide him or her with valuable contacts in the field.

Graduates can explore job opportunities with a wide variety of employers, from the university research branch of psychology or sport sciences to the world of elite athletes. Finding work with the latter, however, can prove extremely difficult.

ADVANCEMENT

Sport psychologists advance in several ways, but primarily by increasing the scope and caliber of their reputations in the field. This is accomplished, of course, by consistently helping athletes to improve their athletic performance and to reduce the emotional and/or mental strain placed upon them. Advancement might come in the form of a new position (working for a professional team) or it might come in the form of a solid private practice.

Sport psychologists who make their living largely in the academic world do so by successfully publishing the results of studies, research, or theories in specialized medical journals.

EARNINGS

Specific salary figures for sport psychologists are not readily available. In general, psychologists' salaries depend on the area of their expertise, the location of their practice, and whether or not they practice alone or in a partnership. The U.S. Department of Labor reports that median annual earnings for all psychologists were $59,440 in 2006. The lowest paid 10 percent earned less than $35,280, and the highest paid 10 percent earned more than $102,730. Be forewarned, however, that with the higher salary comes long years of study in order to attain the educational background necessary to practice. In fact, in order to stay current with topics ranging from treatment to medication, psychologists must continue to learn and study their field for as long as they intend to practice.

WORK ENVIRONMENT

Sport psychologists spend most of their time working in office and hospital environments, but some of their time is spent in the same environments as the athletes they counsel. This may mean spending several hours on a golf course, on a ski slope, or in the gymnasium. Much depends on the type of psychologist. For example, the clinical psychologist would probably spend most of his or her time with athletes in the relative comfort of an office setting and the psychologist would meet with athletes during a regular nine-to-five day. Educational sport psychologists would be more likely to be in the gym or on the golf course, working side-by-side with the rest of the coaching staff. Depending on the nature of the study, a research sport psychologist might spend some time with athletes while they are practicing, but in general, he or she would spend most of the workday in an office or laboratory setting, reviewing or studying the data from his or her studies.

Sport psychologists need to stay up-to-date with developing theories and research. To accomplish this, they may have to spend additional time reading journals, books, and papers; conducting research in the library; or attending conferences on relevant issues. They may need to take additional course work to stay abreast of new theories and techniques, as well as to maintain current certification or licensing. Although sport psychologists spend a lot of time with the athletes they're helping, they also spend large amounts of time working alone.

OUTLOOK

While employment in the general field of psychology in general is likely to grow faster than the average for all occupations through 2014, it is hard to say how this prognosis affects the subspecialty of sport psychology. Largely due to the fact that so much time goes into the training, very few people leave the field entirely. Many stay in the general field of psychology and merely move around, switching specialties, but even this is rare.

While competition is incredibly tough for positions with elite athletes, most experts believe that other areas of sport psychology will continue to offer a substantial number of jobs to new graduates, especially in academe.

Sport psychology can lack the steady income of a private practice or academic teaching post because practitioners are frequently only on call, not steadily billing for their time. It can also be difficult to get work because while they might have a great, famous athlete for a client, chances are pretty good that the athlete doesn't want it known that he or she is getting counseling for a bad marriage, a slump, or a drug problem. This forces the sport psychologist to rely on referrals, which they may not receive all that often when athletes and their agents are trying to keep the athlete's therapy a secret.

FOR MORE INFORMATION

For information on career options in psychology, contact
American Psychological Association
Exercise and Sport Psychology Division
750 First Street, NE
Washington, DC 20002-4242
Tel: 800-374-2721
http://www.apa.org/divisions/div47

For certification info and an overview of the field, visit the About Applied Sport and Exercise Psychology section of the AASP's Web site:
Association for Applied Sport Psychology (AASP)
2810 Crossroads Drive, Suite 3800
Madison, WI 53718-7942
Tel: 608-443-2475
http://www.aaasponline.org

For more information on sport psychology, contact
North American Society for the Psychology of Sport and
Physical Activity
http://www.naspspa.org

INTERVIEW

Dr. Tami Eggleston is an associate professor of psychology at McKendree University in Lebanon, Illinois. She discussed the field of sport psychology with the editors of Careers in Focus: Sports.

Q. What made you become interested in sport psychology?

A. All my life I have been interested in sports. I am currently the crew chief for my husband's big block Chevy rear engine dragster and we drag race around the Midwest. My father was a drag racer, and I always loved the thrill of the competition and the mental side of sports. In high school, I was a cheerleader and loved watching and cheering for basketball, football, and wrestling. In college I studied psychology and went to graduate school in social psychology (the study of people in groups). Finally, I was able to combine all of my interests and started to study sport psychology.

Q. Tell us about your interests in sport psychology and McKendree's program.

A. I teach psychology classes including sport psychology at McKendree University. In addition, I write a monthly column for a magazine for drag racers about the psychology of drag racing. Moreover, I conduct team building and mental performance enhancement workshops for some of McKendree's sport teams including the volleyball, soccer, bowling, and softball teams. I enjoy working with the student athletes one on one or with the entire team. Some of the topics I especially enjoy covering include team building, confidence, stress management, goal setting, and positive self-talk.

At McKendree University we have a sport psychology minor, and students will usually major in psychology, athletic training, business, or physical education. Some universities have a sport psychology major, but currently we believe the minor works well with the more general majors.

Q. What are a few things that young people may not know about a career in sport psychology?

A. I think sometimes the job sounds really "glamorous." For example, I think most people dream of working with a professional athlete or an Olympic athlete. But the truth is that currently there are very few people who are 100 percent sport psychologists. They are more likely to have another job such as being a professor, coach, or athletic trainer, and then they have the training to work in the field of sport psychology.

The other thing is the importance and difficulty of becoming a certified sport psychology consultant. Some people may call themselves a sport psychologist but not really have the appropriate training. Just as you would not want a doctor, a dentist, or a teacher working without the correct credentials, someone should not call themselves a sport psychologist unless they are a psychologist with the correct training. I have gone through the Association for Applied Sport Psychology's certification program, and I am a certified sport psychology consultant.

I also think many people may think that a sport psychologist or consultant would make a lot of money. But again, very few people in the field work with professional teams and athletes so the money is more typical of other jobs in the teaching and helping fields.

Q. What types of students pursue sport psychology study in your program?

A. Most students at McKendree University are psychology, biology, athletic training, or business majors. They are all students who enjoy psychology and also enjoy sports. They tend to be hard working students who enjoy working with others, have good communication skills, enjoy research, and are willing to study and work hard. A lot of our students will also do internships or job shadow to learn more about the field.

Q. What are the most important personal and professional qualities for sport psychology students?

A. Most students at McKendree University primarily want to help others and also love sports. Most of the students either played sports or enjoy watching sports. They also are willing to work hard in college and take classes such as introduction to psychology, health, sport psychology, and other classes related to biology or athletic training. The students also realize that they will probably have to get a bachelor's degree and then go on for at least a master's degree to really do what they want to do. They will also have to have patience in the fact that they may have to do something else for a while before they find their "dream" job. And they also have to be high energy with excellent people skills. Finally, they need to be caring, good listeners, and constantly be willing to learn new things. Having a good sense of humor can also help. A quote that I have heard at sport psychology conferences is, "People have to know you care before they care what you know."

Sports Agents

OVERVIEW

Sports agents act as representatives for professional athletes in many different types of negotiations, providing advice and representation concerning contracts, endorsement and advertisement deals, public appearances, and financial investments and taxes, among other areas. They may represent only one athlete or many, depending on the sport, the size of their agency, and the demands of the client or clients they represent. There are approximately 11,000 agents employed in the United States. However, that figure includes literary and talent agents, as well as sport agents.

HISTORY

People have been entertained by the spectacular feats and athletic skills of individuals and teams even before gladiators performed in front of thousands in the Colosseum in ancient Rome. In the 20th and 21st centuries, sports has consumed a large share of people's free time. Sports figures, like movie stars, have become internationally recognized figures, renowned not only for their athletic prowess, but also for their charismatic personalities. Instead of closing deals with a simple handshake, sports teams now "sign" new actors and ath-

QUICK FACTS

School Subjects
Business
Speech

Personal Skills
Leadership/management

Work Environment
Primarily indoors
One location with some
    travel

Minimum Education Level
Bachelor's degree

Salary Range
$28,870 to $64,500 to
    $114,400+

Certification or Licensing
Recommended

Outlook
Faster than the average

DOT
191

GOE
01.01.01

NOC
5124

O*NET-SOC
13-1011.00

letes to contracts. Like movie stars, athletes began to realize the need to have talented representation—or agents—to protect and promote their interests during contract negotiations. The role of a sports agent has expanded to include many more duties than contract negotiation, although that area remains a crucial responsibility. Today, sports agents handle most, if not all, aspects of a professional athlete's career, from commercial endorsements to financial investments to postretirement career offers.

THE JOB

The sports agent's primary duties consist of negotiating contracts and finding endorsements for his or her clients. Contract negotiations require great communication skills on the part of the sports agent. He or she must clearly summarize the athlete's salary and benefit requirements and have a clear vision of the athlete's future—and how any given contract might affect it. Agents usually represent their clients for the duration of their clients' careers, which sometimes means finding work for athletes once their athletic careers are over. For example, an agent may be able to build into the contract a coaching position, in the event that athlete is injured or otherwise unable to complete the contract. Having a good sense of timing helps the agent as well. Part of understanding a bargaining situation means knowing when to stand your ground and when to cut a deal.

Endorsements and public appearance deals bring additional income to the athlete, but they also have the potential to create a great deal of media attention around the athlete. It is the role of the sports agent to ensure that this media attention is positive and works to the benefit of the athlete. Marketing the public image of an athlete is increasingly difficult in today's media-saturated world; in the past, all an athlete needed to do to be considered a winner was be successful at his or her sport. Today, an athlete who wants to attract top endorsements and public appearances must have incredible charisma and a blemish-free image in addition to being a top athletic performer. Generally speaking, agents must be extremely careful when choosing endorsements for their clients.

Often, a great deal of "schmoozing" is necessary to achieve the kind of contacts that will help clients. For example, an agent for a tennis player might court the attention of executives whose companies manufacture items related to tennis, like tennis racquets, balls, and clothing. By developing friendly business relationships with these individuals, the agent has a direct line to those in charge of dispersing product endorsements. If those companies decide to use an athlete to help promote their products, the agent's athlete hopefully will be the first considered. Networking like this is part of the sports agent's everyday work routine. In between reviewing contracts and financial arrangements, he or she might be on the phone, chatting to an advertiser, scheduling lunch with a sports scout to uncover fresh talent, or handling some other aspect of the athlete's life, such as renting an apartment for the athlete during spring training.

Financial advising is a growing part of the agent's job. Successful new athletes suddenly have a great deal of money. In order to manage those funds, the agent needs to know a reliable financial adviser or act as the athlete's financial adviser. Creating or finding tax shelters, investing money, and preparing for the athlete's retirement are all duties that agents routinely perform for their clients.

Other duties, which are sometimes so small and trivial as to be deceptively insignificant, are many times what keeps a client happy and convinced that the agent has only the client's best interests in mind. This might mean making sure the athlete's mother always has a great seat at home games, or pestering a talk-show host for months to schedule the agent's client for a post-game interview on a popular sports radio program.

REQUIREMENTS

High School

High school courses that will be helpful include business, mathematics, English, and speech. Business courses will provide the financial knowledge an agent needs to act as financial adviser and contract negotiator.

Postsecondary Training

No educational requirements exist for sports agents, but it is increasingly difficult to enter the field without at least a bachelor's degree in business administration, marketing, or sports management. Many who eventually become agents also go on to pursue a graduate degree in law or business, two areas that increase but do not guarantee your chances at success. Contract law and economics are courses that can help an agent improve the client's chances, and his or her own chances, for successful negotiations.

Certification or Licensing

Many sports agents obtain a license or professional registration as demonstration of their commitment and integrity. Although these are not yet mandatory, it is one way for athletes to determine who, among agents, is legitimate and therefore a better person to hire. Agents working for clients who belong to unions, such as the National Football League Players Association, are required to obtain a union franchise. Basically, the franchise is an agreement between the agent and the athlete's union in which the agent promises to abide by the standards created by the union to protect its members. All licenses, registrations, and franchises are easily obtained by paying a filing fee and do not represent a real challenge to the sports agent.

Other Requirements

Contacts and exposure to athletes are the unofficial requirements for sports agents. Simply put, without knowing or having access

Books to Read

Baine, Celeste. *High Tech Hot Shots: Careers in Sports Engineering.* Alexandria, Va.: National Society of Professional Engineers, 2004.

Buren, Jodi. *Superwomen: 100 Women-100 Sports.* New York: Bulfinch Press, 2004.

Heitzmann, William Ray, and Mark Rowh. *Careers for Sports Nuts & Other Athletic Types.* New York: McGraw Hill, 2004.

Hofstetter, Adam. *Cool Careers Without College for People Who Love Sports.* New York: Rosen Publishing Group, 2007.

Kilduff, Mike. *The Passion for Sports: Athletes Tell Their Stories of Why They Love Their Games.* New York: Sporting News Books, 2002.

Miller, Ernestine. *Making Her Mark: Firsts and Milestones in Women's Sports.* New York: McGraw-Hill, 2002.

Ribas, J. Michael. *Careers in Entertainment and Sports.* San Francisco: WetFeet Inc., 2006.

Wilson, Robert F. *Careers in Sports, Fitness, and Recreation.* Hauppauge, N.Y.: Barron's Educational Series, 2001.

to athletes, it is next to impossible to represent them. Insiders say that often, a successful agent's first client is his or her college roommate—later hired when the college athlete turned professional.

The sports industry generates revenue in the hundreds of billions of dollars, only a portion of which actually goes to the athlete, so everyone who comes to the bargaining table—from management to athlete to advertiser—has a lot at stake. Sports agents must be able to handle tension and stress well, arguing effectively for their client's interests whether the opponent is the head of an international shoe manufacturer or the local real estate agent trying to sell the athlete a new house.

Finally, a large part of the sports agent's job is talking, making contacts, and then using those contacts to improve a client's position. This type of interaction is the bread and butter of a sports agent's career. As one insider put it, being just this side of annoying, obnoxious, or brash helps in this business. Often, the agent with the most name recognition is the one who ends up with the job.

EXPLORING

Finding jobs in this field is as challenging for those just starting out as it is for those at the top. Even intern positions and entry-level jobs are hard to get, because so many people are struggling to enter the field. Insiders recommend starting as early as possible and taking any job that gives you exposure to athletes. High school students can start by shagging balls at tennis tournaments, golf caddying, or applying for coveted ballboy/girl and batboy/girl or clubhouse assistant positions with major league teams.

College internships are probably the most valuable introduction to the field, especially when you consider that many of the top management firms that hire agents do not accept younger applicants. These firms are looking for men and women who are eager and willing to learn about the field. Insiders believe the internship is crucial to getting a solid start because it may be the last time when anyone will let you close enough to see how the job is done; once someone passes the internship stage, they are viewed by other agents as competition and the avenues of communication close up. Although young recruits in an agency receive some informal training on the job, the secrets of the trade are highly individualized and are developed by the truly successful among the agents.

EMPLOYERS

Agents are employed by the professional athletes they represent. They are also employed by top management firms, such as International Management Group.

STARTING OUT

If you do not know an athlete, have no connections or access to athletes, and have had no experience prior to applying to agencies, chances are you will find yourself changing fields pretty quickly. Just as there are no professional organizations and no formal training to do this job, there is no one way to do it, which only makes getting started more difficult. The best way of breaking into the field is to start early and obtain a good internship—one that gives you some exposure to agents and athletes, as well as a chance to develop those contacts. Add to this any information or hot tips you might have on new, fresh talent and you may have a chance. International Management Group, a top employer of sports agents, has summer and semester internship programs for young people interested in this career. For more information, visit http://www.imgworld.com.

Most people who become agents get involved with a sport, either because they once played it, or a sibling did, or they have followed it so closely as to have made important or solid contacts in the field. Coaches, scouts, and the athletes themselves would all be considered good contacts. So, too, are newscasters, athletic trainers, even physicians; in short, anyone who can introduce you to athletes is a potential contact.

ADVANCEMENT

In the field of sports management, advancement comes with success, the formula for which is pretty straightforward; if an agent's athletes are successful (and the agent handles the careers of those athletes well), then the agent is successful—financially as well as in terms of reputation. A good, solid reputation will, in turn, garner that agent more successful clients.

EARNINGS

Sports agents can earn phenomenal amounts of money by representing a single star athlete like LeBron James, Venus Williams, or Tiger Woods. Athletes of this stature earn $50 million a year or more in salary and endorsements. A 5 percent commission on such earnings would net the agent approximately $2.5 million a year. Agent commissions, or percentages, at top management firms run anywhere from 5 to 10 percent of the player's earnings, and up to 25 percent for endorsements the agency negotiates on behalf of the athlete.

Although these are high salaries, anyone interested in pursuing a career in this field should understand that most of the athletes the typical sports agent represents are not of the rare star-like variety. This means that they will earn significantly less than agents who represent premier athletes. According to the U.S. Department of Labor, agents of all types (including literary and actors' agents as well as sports agents) earned a median annual salary of $64,500 in 2006. The lowest 10 percent earned $28,870 or less, while the highest 25 percent earned $114,400 or more annually. According to one insider, the sky's the limit; if an agent is extremely ambitious and the agent's contacts within the sports world are fruitful, he or she can earn well over a million dollars a year. People entering the field of sports management should know the realities of the job—the million-dollar scenario is as likely for agents as it is for athletes. It takes ambition, talent, timing, and lots of luck to make it big in this field. Enjoyment of the work, then, is crucial to job satisfaction.

WORK ENVIRONMENT

Sports agents work with athletes in various stages of their careers, often before those careers even take off. Agents may spend time with the athlete at practice, hours on the telephone in the office, a day or two scouting new talent, and lunches and dinners with potential advertisers or employers of the athlete.

Sports agents spend most of their time on the telephone, arranging meetings, discussing prospects, networking connections, keeping in touch with the industry trends and issues, and most of all, speaking with their client about strategies and whatever problems the client is dealing with, from negotiating a raise in salary to helping the player through a slump.

OUTLOOK

The outlook for sports agents, in general, is very favorable. The U.S. Department of Labor predicts faster-than-average growth for agents over the next decade, mainly because the sports industry is thriving and there is nothing to suggest that the public's interest in it will dwindle. The increasing popularity of women's sports leagues, such as the Women's National Basketball Association, also accounts for the rapid growth in this field. Also, as cable television brings greater choices to the viewer, it is possible that less-publicized sports will gain in popularity through the increased exposure, thus breathing life and revenues into those sports and creating new demand.

FOR MORE INFORMATION

No professional organizations or associations exist for sports agents. Some sports management programs teach courses on the subject. However, for the most part, an agent has to learn the ropes by observing the successes and mistakes of others, developing his or her own strategies, techniques, and contacts along the way. Insiders report that while established agents will often discuss their work with others, divulging contacts and secrets of the trade is simply not done. The following is one of the top management firms in the country, a good source for internships and jobs, as well as leads to other companies:

International Management Group
IMG Center
1360 East 9th Street, Suite 100
Cleveland, OH 44114-1782
Tel: 216-522-1200
http://www.imgworld.com

Sports Broadcasters and Announcers

OVERVIEW

Sports broadcasters, or *sportscasters*, for radio and television stations select, write, and deliver footage of current sports news for the sports segment of radio and television news broadcasts or for specific sports events, channels, or shows. They may provide pre- and postgame coverage of sports events, including interviews with coaches and athletes, as well as play-by-play coverage during the game or event.

Sports announcers are the official voices of the teams. At home games, the sports announcer makes pre-game announcements, introduces the players in the starting lineups, and keeps the spectators in the stadium or arena abreast of the details of the game by announcing such things as fouls, substitutions, and goals, and who is making them.

HISTORY

Radio signals, first transmitted by Guglielmo Marconi in 1895, led to early experimentation with broadcasting in the years preceding World War I. After the war began, however, a ban on non-military radio broadcasts delayed radio's acceptance. In 1919, when the ban was lifted, hundreds of amateur stations sprang up. By 1922, 500 were licensed by the government. Codes and domestic broadcast wavelengths were assigned by the government, which created a traffic jam of aerial signals. Eventually, more powerful stations were permitted to broadcast at a higher wavelength, provided these stations only broadcast live music. This move by the government quickly brought entertainment from large, urban areas to the small towns and rural areas that characterized most of the United States at the time.

In the early days of radio broadcasts, anyone who operated the station would read, usually verbatim, news stories from the day's paper. Quickly, station managers realized that the station's "voice" needed as much charisma and flair as possible. Announcers and journalists with good speaking voices were hired. With the arrival of television, many of those who worked in radio broadcasting moved to this new medium.

Corporate-sponsored radio stations weren't long in coming; Westinghouse Corporation and American Telephone and Telegraph (AT&T) raced to enter the market. Westinghouse engineer Frank Conrad received a license for what is viewed as the first modern radio station, KDKA, in Pittsburgh, Pennsylvania. KDKA broadcast music programs, the 1920 presidential election, and sports events. The next year, Westinghouse began to sell radio sets for as little as $25. By 1924, the radio-listening public numbered 20 million.

Meanwhile, as early as 1929, Vladimir Kosma Zworykin, a Soviet immigrant employed by Westinghouse, was experimenting with visual images to create an all-electronic television system. By 1939, the system was demonstrated at the New York's World Fair with none other than President Franklin D. Roosevelt speaking before the camera. World War II and battles over government regulation and AM and FM frequencies interrupted the introduction of television to the American public, but by 1944, the government had determined specific frequencies for both FM radio and television.

In 1946, there were 6,000 television sets in use; by 1951, the number had risen to an astonishing 12 million sets. The stage had been set for a battle between radio and television. In the ensuing years, expert after expert predicted the demise of radio. The popularity of television, with its soap operas, family dramas, and game shows, was believed by nearly everyone to be too strong a competitor for the old-fashioned, sound-only aspect of radio. The experts were proved wrong; radio continues to flourish.

The national radio networks of the early days are gone, but satellites allow local stations to broadcast network shows anywhere with the equipment to receive the satellite link. The development of filmed and videotaped television, cable, and satellite transmissions, broadcasting deregulation, and an international market through direct broadcast satellite systems has drastically changed the face and future of both radio and television.

Today's sports broadcasters in radio and television have all these technological tools and more at their fingertips. Want to see an instant replay of the game-winning three-point shot by Kobe Bryant? As the sportscaster describes it, a technician is playing it back for the viewing public. Have to travel to Costa Rica for a business trip, but hate to miss that Yankees game? No problem. A sportscaster is giving the play-by-play to an AM network station that is, in turn, sending it via satellite to a Costa Rican client-station.

THE JOB

One of the primary jobs of most sportscasters for both radio and television stations is to determine what sports news to carry during a news segment. The sportscaster begins working on the first broadcast by reading the sports-related clippings that come in over the various news wire services, such as Associated Press and United Press International. To follow up on one of these stories, the sportscaster might telephone several contacts, such as a coach, scout, or athlete, to see if he or she can get a comment or more information. The sportscaster also might want to prepare a list of upcoming games, matches, and other sports events. Athletes often make public appearances for charity events and the sportscaster might want to include a mention of the charity and the participating athlete or athletes.

After deciding which stories to cover and the lineup of the stories that will be featured in the first of the day's broadcasts, sportscasters then review any audio or video clips that will accompany the various stories. Sportscasters working for radio stations choose audio clips, usually interviews, that augment the piece of news they will read. Sportscasters working for television stations look for video footage—the best 10 seconds of this game or that play—to demonstrate why a certain team lost or won. Sometimes sportscasters choose footage that is humorous or poignant to illustrate the point of the news item.

After they decide which audio or video segments to use, sportscasters then work with sound or video editors to edit the data into a reel or video, or they edit the footage into a tape themselves. In either case, the finished product will be handed over to the news director or producer with a script detailing when it should play. The news producer or director will make certain that the reel or video comes in on cue during the broadcast.

Frequently a sportscaster will make brief appearances at local sports events to interview coaches and players before and after the game and sometimes during breaks in the action. These interviews, as well as any footage of the game that the station's camera crews obtain, are then added to the stock from which sportscasters choose for their segments.

Usually, the main broadcast for both radio and television sportscasters is the late-evening broadcast following the evening's scheduled programming. This is when most of the major league sports events have concluded, the statistics for the game are released, and final official scores are reported. Any changes that have occurred since the day's first sports broadcast are updated and new footage or sound bites are added. The final newscast for a television sportscaster will most likely include highlights from the day's sports events, especially dramatic shots of the most impressive or winning points scored.

In televised sports news, the emphasis is on image. Often sportscasters, like other newscasters, are only on camera for several seconds at a time, but their voices continue over the videotape that highlights unique moments in different games.

For many sportscasters who work in television, preparing the daily sportscasts is their main job and takes up most of their time. For others, especially sportscasters who work in radio, delivering a play-by-play broadcast of particular sports events is the main focus of their job. These men and women use their knowledge of the game or sport to create a visual picture of the game for radio listeners with words, as it is happening. The most common sports for which sportscasters deliver play-by-play broadcasts are baseball, basketball, football, and hockey. A few sportscasters broadcast horse races from the racetrack and sometimes these broadcasts are carried by off-track betting facilities.

Sportscasters who give the play-by-play for a basketball game, for example, usually arrive an hour or so before the start of the game. Often they have a pregame show that features interviews with, and a statistical review of, the competing teams and athletes. To broadcast a basketball game, sportscasters sit courtside in a special media section so that they can see the action up close. During football, baseball, and hockey games sportscasters usually sit in one of the nearby media boxes. Throughout the game sportscasters narrate each play for radio listeners using rapid, precise, and lively descriptions. During time-outs, halftimes, or other breaks in play, sportscasters might deliver their own running commentaries of the game, the players' performances, and the coaching.

A sportscaster who specializes in play-by-play broadcasts needs to have an excellent mastery of the rules, players, and statistics of a sport, as well as the hand signals officials use to regulate the flow of a game. Some sportscasters provide play-by-play broadcasts for several different teams or sports, from college to professional levels, requiring them to know more than one sport or team well.

Some sportscasters, who are often former athletes or established sports personalities, combine two aspects of the job. They act as *anchors* or *co-anchors* for sports shows and give some play-by-play commentary. They may also provide their television or radio audience with statistics and general updates.

Sports announcers provide spectators with public address announcements before and during a sports event. For this job, announcers must remain utterly neutral, simply delivering the facts— goals scored, numbers of fouls, or a time-out taken. Sports announcers may be sportscasters or they may be *professional announcers* or *emcees* who make their living recording voice-overs for radio and television commercials and for businesses or stores.

Sports announcers usually give the lineups for games, provide player names and numbers during specific times in a contest, make public announcements during time-outs and pauses in play, and generally keep the crowd involved in the event (especially in baseball). *Baseball announcers* may try to rally the crowd or start the crowd singing or doing the wave.

REQUIREMENTS

High School

Graduating from high school is an important first step on the road to becoming a sports broadcaster or announcer. While in school, take classes that will allow you to work on your speaking and writing skills. Classes in speech, English, journalism, and foreign languages, such as Spanish and French, will be helpful. You may also find it helpful to take courses in drama and computer science.

Postsecondary Training

Educational requirements for sportscasting positions vary depending on the position. Competition for radio and television sports broadcasting positions is especially fierce, so any added edge can make the difference.

Television sportscasters who deliver the news in sports usually have bachelor's degrees in communications or journalism. However, personality, charisma, and overall on-camera appearance are so important to ratings that station executives often pay closer attention to the taped auditions they receive from prospective sportscasters than to the items on resumes. Prepare for the job by learning a sport inside and out, developing valuable contacts in the field through internships and part-time or volunteer jobs, and earning a degree in journalism or communications. It also should be noted that the industry is finicky and subjective about looks and charisma.

It is not as crucial for sportscasters who deliver play-by-play broadcasts for radio stations to have the journalistic skills that a television

A broadcaster interviews NASCAR driver David Gilliland at Talladega Speedway in Alabama. *(Jeff Greenberg, The Image Works)*

sportscaster has, although good interviewing skills are essential. Instead, they need excellent verbal skills, a daunting command of the sport or sports that they will be covering, and a familiarity with the competing players, coaches, and team histories. To draw a complete picture for their listeners, sportscasters often reach back into history for an interesting detail or statistic, so a good memory for statistics and trivia involving sports history is helpful.

Other Requirements
A nice speaking voice, excellent verbal and interviewing skills, a pleasant appearance, a solid command of sports in general as well as in-depth knowledge of the most popular sports (football, basketball, baseball, and hockey), and an outgoing personality are all necessary for a successful career in sportscasting.

In addition, you need to have a strong voice, excellent grammar and English usage, and the ability to ad-lib if necessary.

EXPLORING
High school and college students have many opportunities to investigate this career choice, but the most obvious way is to participate in a sport. By learning a sport inside and out, you can gain valuable

insight into the movements and techniques that, as a sportscaster, you will be describing. In addition, firsthand experience and a love of the sport itself makes it easier to remember interesting trivia related to the sport and the names and numbers of the pros who play it.

If you do not have the coordination or skill for the sport itself, you can volunteer to help out with the team by shagging balls, running drills, or keeping statistics. The latter is perhaps the best way to learn the percentages and personal athletic histories of athletes.

An excellent way to develop the necessary communications skills is to take a journalism course, join the school's speech or debate team, deliver the morning announcements, work as a DJ on the school radio station, or volunteer at a local radio station or cable television station.

John Earnhardt from the National Association of Broadcasters has this advice: "Write about your school's sports teams for your school newspaper or hometown newspaper and read, read, read about sports. Knowledge about the area you are interested in reporting about is the best tool for success. It is also necessary to be able to express yourself well through the spoken word. Speaking before an audience can be the best practice for speaking before the camera or on a microphone."

Finally, you can hone your sportscasting skills on your own while watching your favorite sports event by turning down the sound on your television and tape-recording your own play-by-play deliveries.

EMPLOYERS

Most sports broadcasters work for television networks or radio stations. The large sports networks also employ many broadcasters. John Earnhardt says, "The main employers of sports broadcasters are sports networks that own the rights to broadcast sporting events and the broadcast stations themselves." Radio sportscasters are hired by radio stations that range from small stations to mega-stations.

Sports announcers work for professional sports arenas, sports teams, minor league and major league ball teams, colleges, universities, and high schools.

Because sports are popular all over the country, there are opportunities everywhere, although the smaller the town the fewer the opportunities. "Larger cities generally have more opportunities because of the number of stations and the number of sports teams that need to be covered," Earnhardt says.

STARTING OUT

Although an exceptional audition tape might land you an on-camera or on-air job, most sportscasters get their start by writing copy, answering phones, operating cameras or equipment, or assisting the sportscaster with other jobs. Internships or part-time jobs will give you the opportunity to become comfortable in front of a camera or behind a microphone. Of course, contacts within the industry come in handy. In many cases, it is simply an individual's devotion to the sport and the job that makes the difference—that and being in the right place at the right time. John Earnhardt adds that knowledge is key as well. "It obviously helps to know the sport you are reporting on—first, one needs to study the sport and know the sport's rules, history, and participants better than anyone," he advises.

Put together an audiotape (if you are applying for a radio job or an announcer position) or a videotape or DVD (for television jobs) that showcases your abilities. On the tape, give your account of the sports events that took place on a certain day.

ADVANCEMENT

In the early stages of their careers, sportscasters might advance from a sports copywriter position to become an actual broadcaster. Later in their careers, sportscasters advance by moving to larger and larger markets, beginning with local television stations and advancing to one of the major networks.

Sportscasters who work in radio may begin in a similar way; advancement for these individuals might come in the form of a better time slot for a sports show, or the chance to give more commentary.

Sports announcers advance by adding to the number of teams for whom they provide public address announcements. Some sports announcers also may start out working for colleges and minor leagues and then move up to major league work.

EARNINGS

Salaries in sportscasting vary, depending on the medium (radio or television), the market (large or small, commercial or public), and whether the sportscaster is a former athlete or recognized sports celebrity, as opposed to a newcomer trying to carve out a niche.

According to the U.S. Department of Labor, the average salary of radio and television announcers was $24,310 in 2006. Salaries ranged from less than $13,620 to $68,600 or more. A 2007 salary survey by the Radio-Television News Directors Association found that television sports anchors earned average salaries of $52,300.

Sportscasting jobs in radio tend to pay less than those in television. Beginners will find jobs more easily in smaller stations, but the pay will be correspondingly lower than it is in larger markets. The average salary for a radio sportscaster, according to a 2007 survey by the survey by the Radio-Television News Directors Association, was $31,300.

Salaries are usually higher for former athletes and recognized sports personalities or celebrities, such as ex-coaches like John Madden. These individuals already have an established personality within the sports community and may thus have an easier time getting athletes and coaches to talk to them. Salaries for such recognizable personalities can be $2 million or more per year.

WORK ENVIRONMENT

Sportscasters usually work in clean, well-lighted booths or sets in radio or television studios. They also work in special soundproof media rooms at the sports facility that hosts sports events.

Time constraints and deadlines can create havoc and add stress to an already stressful job; often a sportscaster has to race back to the studio to make the final evening broadcast. Sportscasters who deliver play-by-play commentary for radio listeners have the very stressful job of describing everything going on in a game as it happens. They cannot take their eyes off the ball and the players while the clock is running, and this can be nerve-wracking and stressful.

On the other hand, sportscasters are usually on a first-name basis with some of the most famous people in the world, namely, professional athletes. They quickly lose the star-struck quality that usually afflicts most spectators and must learn to ask well-developed, concise, and sometimes difficult questions of coaches and athletes.

Sports announcers usually sit in press boxes near the action so they can have a clear view of players and their numbers when announcing. Depending on the type of sport, this may be an enclosed area or they may be out in the open air. Sports announcers start announcing before the event begins and close the event with more announcements, but then are able to end their workday. Because sporting events are scheduled at many different times of the day, announcers sometimes must be available at odd hours.

OUTLOOK

Competition for jobs in sportscasting will continue to be fierce, with the better paying, jobs in larger markets going to experienced sportscasters who have proven they can keep ratings high. Sportscasters who can easily substitute for other on-camera newscasters or anchors may be more employable.

Employment for sports broadcasters and announcers is expected to grow more slowly than the average for all occupations through 2014 because not that many new radio and television stations are expected to enter the market. Most of the job openings will come as sportscasters leave the market to retire, relocate, or enter other professions. In general, employment in this field is not affected by economic recessions or declines; in the event of cutbacks, the on-camera sports broadcasters and announcers are the last to go.

FOR MORE INFORMATION

To read more about the sportscasting field, including current news, interviews with working professionals, and profiles of all-time sportscasting greats, visit

American Sportscasters Association
225 Broadway, Suite 2030
New York, NY 10007-3001
Tel: 212-227-8080
http://www.americansportscastersonline.com

The AWSM is a membership organization of women and men employed in sports writing, editing, broadcast and production, public relations, and sports information. Visit its Web site for information on internships and scholarships.

Association for Women in Sports Media (AWSM)
PO Box F
Bayville, NJ 08721-0317
http://www.awsmonline.org

For a list of schools that offer programs and courses in broadcasting, contact

Broadcast Education Association
1771 N Street, NW
Washington, DC 20036-2891
Tel: 202-429-5355
Email: beainfo@beaweb.org
http://www.beaweb.org

For information on FCC licenses, contact
Federal Communications Commission (FCC)
445 12th Street, SW
Washington, DC 20554-2101
Tel: 888-225-5322
Email: fccinfo@fcc.gov
http://www.fcc.gov

For general information about broadcasting, contact
National Association of Broadcasters
1771 N Street, NW
Washington, DC 20036-2891
Tel: 202-429-5300
Email: nab@nab.org
http://www.nab.org

For career information and helpful Internet links, contact
Radio-Television News Directors Association
1600 K Street, NW, Suite 700
Washington, DC 20006-2838
Tel: 202-659-6510
Email: rtnda@rtnda.org
http://www.rtnda.org

Sports Equipment Managers

OVERVIEW

Sports equipment managers are responsible for maintaining, ordering, and inventorying athletic equipment and apparel. They deal with everything from fitting football shoulder pads to sharpening hockey skates to doing the team's laundry. There are more than 800 equipment managers employed in the United States, with the majority working for collegiate and high school teams.

HISTORY

Sports cannot be played without using some sort of equipment. Keeping that equipment in good working condition and safe for players to use is the job of equipment managers. One of the major reasons for the emergence of professional equipment managers was the need for qualified athletic personnel to fit football helmets, according to the Athletic Equipment Managers Association (AEMA). It was not until the advent of the plastic shell helmet, which contributed to a more intense-contact game, that the number of injuries in sports rose. The National Operating Committee on Standards for Athletic Equipment began developing standards for football helmets. This increased attention also focused on the need for properly fitted equipment and specially trained personnel to perform the sizing. The AEMA was formed in 1974 when "a handful of equipment managers got together to discuss how to promote our profession and enhance the protection of student athletes involved in football," says Terry Schlatter, former

AEMA president and head athletic equipment manager, University of Wisconsin–Madison.

THE JOB

The responsibilities of equipment managers vary greatly, depending on whether they work for high schools, colleges, universities, or professional teams. Duties are also different from sport to sport, because some have more participants than others. "My responsibilities include budgeting for all of the university's sports and requisitioning of equipment," says Terry Schlatter. "Some equipment managers might not do anything with budgets and might just fit football equipment and do laundry." Other duties include purchasing, maintenance, administration and organization, management, professional relations and education, and keeping inventory of all the equipment.

Sports equipment managers are responsible for ordering all the equipment (including uniforms) for their team or school's sports programs. Once the equipment arrives, they make sure that it properly fits each player. Poorly fitting equipment or uniforms can cause discomfort, a lack of mobility, a reduction of vision or hearing, and even injury. After use, equipment managers keep the equipment in good working order. They inspect and clean each piece of equipment to ensure that it meets safety standards. Equipment managers are also responsible for equipment control, which includes pre- and postseason inventory, use, and storage.

"Duties also might include (but are not limited to) facility scheduling, maintaining relationships with vendors, keeping up-to-date on current trends and products available, compliance with the National Collegiate Athletic Association and conference rule changes regarding uniforms and equipment, and game day management," says Sam Trusner, equipment manager at Millikin University.

Equipment managers need good communication and personnel management skills because they work with coaches, athletic directors, and their staffs. "The best part of the job is working with the athletes and coaches," Terry Schlatter says. "The worst is the hours and that you receive very little recognition for what you do because you work behind the scenes."

REQUIREMENTS

High School

High school courses that will be helpful include computer science, mathematics, and business. Serving as the equipment manager of one of your high school athletic teams or clubs will give you a great introduction to work in this field.

Postsecondary Training

To become a professional equipment manager, the AEMA suggests one of the following paths: (1) high school/GED degree and five years of paid, nonstudent employment in athletic equipment management; (2) four-year college degree and two years paid, nonstudent employment in athletic equipment management; or (3) four-year college degree and 1,800 hours as a student equipment manager. Terry Schlatter recommends taking some business classes to help you prepare to handle equipment budgets and negotiate contracts with manufacturers such as Nike, Reebok, and Adidas. The AEMA offers a scholarship program to help with college expenses.

Certification or Licensing

The AEMA began a professional certification program in 1991. There are more than 500 certified equipment managers in the United States and Canada. To obtain certification, equipment managers must be 21 years of age and be a member in good standing with the AEMA, and complete one of the three requirements listed in the previous section. Once these requirements have been met, candidates must take and pass a certification examination. The certification process also includes continuing education, such as annual conventions, workshops, seminars, and meetings.

Other Requirements

"Equipment managers must have excellent organizational skills and the ability to get along with many people," Sam Trusner says. "They also must be able to take criticism, be creative and responsible, have basic computer skills, and, most of all, have patience." To these qualities, Terry Schlatter adds the willingness to work a lot of overtime. "Football people work between 70 and 80 hours a week during the season," he says.

EMPLOYERS

High schools, colleges, universities, and professional sports teams throughout the country hire equipment managers, although the number of positions with professional teams is limited, and they are very difficult to obtain. Several sports need the help of equipment managers, including football, basketball, baseball, hockey, and lacrosse.

STARTING OUT

"I started out doing laundry, then went to fitting shoes and helmets," says Terry Schlatter. "Then I was responsible for ordering all of the football equipment. From there, I became head equipment manager and was responsible for ordering equipment for all of the sports, as well as football. Now I handle budgeting for all of the sports, as well as Reebok contract operations."

Some equipment managers began exploring the field in high school, where they served as volunteers for their sports teams. Others worked in that position in college, which is helpful for developing contacts for potential employment after graduation.

ADVANCEMENT

"Equipment managers can be promoted to administrative positions within the athletic department, such as athletic directors and administrative assistants. Some also obtain top positions with sporting goods companies," notes Sam Trusner. In this industry, it is important to work your way up through the system. "Not many people walk into head equipment jobs without working their way up through the system or knowing a head coach who promotes them to administration," says Terry Schlatter.

EARNINGS

Salaries range from $20,000 to $60,000 for head equipment manager positions and $15,000 to $40,000 for assistants. Equipment managers' salaries depend a great deal on if they work for a professional team or the local high school.

WORK ENVIRONMENT

Equipment managers spend most of their time in schools or in professional team offices during the off-season. "Travel is generally limited to football," Terry Schlatter adds. "Some schools might have the equipment manager travel with the basketball team. I would say 90 percent of the time is spent on campus."

Equipment managers who work for professional teams usually travel with those teams and coordinate shipping of their team's gear to each game site. Some football equipment managers might also travel to training camp.

OUTLOOK

"The profession is changing rapidly and growing by leaps and bounds for college and university equipment managers," says Sam Trusner. "With the current emphasis on adding more women's sports to comply with Title IX guidelines, there is a shortage of qualified women's equipment managers. AEMA certification has also brought about greater acceptance by administrators for the need to have qualified individuals in these positions. With the addition of computerized inventory programs, university-wide contracts with dealers, and the big-business atmosphere of athletics in general, equipment managers are being called upon to broaden their range of knowledge in many new areas."

FOR MORE INFORMATION

For information on scholarships and certification, contact
Athletic Equipment Managers Association
http://www.aema1.com

For information on sports equipment standards, contact
National Operating Committee on Standards for Athletic Equipment
11020 King Street, Suite 215
Overland Park, KS 66210-1201
http://www.nocsae.org

INTERVIEW

Mike Royster, assistant athletic director for facilities and equipment at the University of Tennessee at Chattanooga and president of the Athletic Equipment Managers Association, discussed his career with the editors of Careers in Focus: Sports.

Q. How long have you been a sports equipment manager? Please tell us about your career.

A. I am in my 34th year at the University of Tennessee at Chattanooga (UTC). Since January of 2000, I have been assistant athletic director for facilities and equipment. My responsibilities include overseeing the equipment purchases and inventory of UTC's 17 intercollegiate athletic programs as well as the repair and maintenance of athletic equipment. I also coordinate travel for the football and men's basketball teams.

I have been a certified athletic equipment manager since July 1991 and have been a member of the Athletic Equipment Managers Association for more than 25 years.

Q. What are your typical tasks/responsibilities?

A. My job is much easier now that I have a full time assistant, but for years I was it. The one thing I have learned over the course of many years is there is no such thing as a typical day, except maybe in the summer months, which now is really just June.

But to help you get an idea of some of my responsibilities in detail, let me walk you through a typical work cycle starting on the Thursday before an away football game to Little Rock, Arkansas:

Thursday

- 6:00–6:05 A.M.: Check messages and get ready to start the day. Walk through the equipment room for a quick check of everything, but mainly laundry. We have to be sure the football team and coaches' laundry is done at night so we can do all the other sports' laundry during the morning.
- 6:00–8:00 A.M.: Make the laundry change over and put away all the laundry that was done the previous night.
- 8:00 A.M.–Noon: Pick up the rental truck for that week's trip. As soon as we return, we load all our trunks and the trainer's equipment. When that is done, we get the passenger van from the motor pool. Then we print a packing check sheet for the players and begin readying their equipment travel bags for packing.
- Noon–1:00 P.M.: Lunch
- 1:00–3:30 P.M.: Student managers arrive as close to 1:00 P.M. as their class schedule will allow. We finish packing and then get the field set up and ready for practice.
- 3:30–5:00 P.M.: Practice
- 5:00–7:00 P.M.: After practice we put everything away, hand out the travel bags, and load the players' bags on the truck. After checking to be sure we have all the players' bags and double-checking our own checklist we head to Arkansas (where our team is playing the game).
- 7:00 P.M.–1:00 A.M.: If we are lucky, we leave by 7:00 P.M. and drive to Memphis, Tennessee (a stopping point on the trip) in around five hours.

Friday

- 10:00 A.M.: Finish the trip to Little Rock, Arkansas.
- Noon: Arrive at Little Rock and War Memorial Stadium.
- Noon–3:00 P.M.: Unload the truck, set-up the dressing room, clean the helmets, and set up the coaches' phones in the press box. During that time we go to the hotel and check in and get all the room keys for the team. Then we set up for practice.
- 3:00–4:30 P.M.: Practice
- 4:30–5:30 P.M.: Hand out room keys to the players/coaches. Clean up after practice and lock up facilities.

Saturday

- 8:00 A.M.: Arrive at the stadium four hours before the game to finish game set-up and be ready for the players' arrival.
- 8:00 A.M.–5:00 P.M.: Set up the field, play the game, collect and load up the equipment.
- 5:00 P.M.: Leave for home
- 12:00 A.M.–???: After a seven- to eight-hour trip home, we unload the truck, wash the uniforms and dirty laundry, repack the trunks, return all the vehicles, clean the game shoes, and get ready to start another workweek Sunday afternoon.

Q. What do you like most and least about your job?

A. The things I like most are easy—the friendships and the young people I come in contact with. Right now I have four young men who worked for me as students who are now doing what I do at other schools. At one time I had seven, but some have moved into other fields. I am very proud of all the young men and women who have honored me with their time and help through the years. I hope in some way that their time with me has helped them in some way. I don't believe any athletic program can survive without student managers and student help, no matter what level. We have tried to make them good students and good people, but if the truth were told I believe they have made my life so much better just because they passed through it.

Second would be all the friends you make along the way. There are some really special people in athletics, and that is because it takes special people. It is not a nine-to-five job. It takes dedication and hard work and there are not a lot of people who are willing to sacrifice their time.

The thing I like least is the selfish athlete or coach you come in contact with every so often. Unfortunately, it is part of the job and you just have to deal with it. I believe it is best to do your job to the best of your ability, bite your tongue, and move on.

Q. What are the three most important professional qualities for sports equipment managers?

A. These are my thoughts, but if you ask 50 people you might get 50 different answers.

Accountability and dependability. With so much money invested by your school in athletic equipment, you must be able to account for everything. In doing this, administrators must have faith in your dependability to get the job done. You will probably have to earn that dependability. The accountability will go hand and hand with number two.

Organization. You must be organized and you need to know how to organize to get the job done. This not only applies to the equipment and equipment room but also your time. I believe if you organize your equipment room, you will be able to walk through it and see if anything is out of place or missing. I have tried to organize my equipment room so that any outsider could come in and find what they are looking for. Do whatever you have to do to help yourself; for example, I have a checklist for everything. It would be a shame to get to a road game and find out you had forgotten the uniforms, and don't think it can't happen, because I have seen it happen to a visiting team.

Keep up with the industry. I believe you must keep abreast of new and changing equipment. You must keep up with rule changes that effect equipment. You should talk to your fellow equipment managers and read the athletic journals and magazines. I believe this is as important as the first two traits.

Sports Executives

OVERVIEW

Sports executives, sometimes known as *team presidents*, *CEOs*, and *general managers*, manage professional, collegiate, and minor league sports teams. They are responsible for the teams' finances, as well as overseeing the other departments within the organization, such as marketing, public relations, accounting, ticket sales, advertising, sponsorship, and community relations. Sports executives also work on establishing long-term contacts and support within the communities where the teams play.

HISTORY

The sports industry has matured into one of the largest industries in the United States. Professional teams are the most widely recognized industry segment in sports. Professional teams include all of the various sports teams, leagues, and governing bodies for which individuals get paid for their performance. Some of the most notable organizations include the National Football League, National Basketball Association, National Hockey League, and Major League Baseball. These are commonly known as the four majors. During recent decades, more professional leagues have started, such as the Women's National Basketball Association, the Arena Football League, and Major League Soccer. There are also many minor league and collegiate organizations.

THE JOB

The two top positions in most sports organizations are *team president* and *general manager*. Depending on the size of the

QUICK FACTS

School Subjects
Business
Physical education

Personal Skills
Communication/ideas
Leadership/management

Work Environment
Primarily indoors
One location with some
  travel

Minimum Education Level
Bachelor's degree

Salary Range
$20,000 to $50,000 to
  $1,000,000+

Certification or Licensing
None available

Outlook
More slowly than the average

DOT
153

GOE
13.01.01

NOC
0513

O*NET-SOC
11-1011.02, 11-1021.00

franchise, these two positions might be blended together and held by one person.

Team presidents are the chief executive officers of the club. They are responsible for the overall financial success of the team. Presidents oversee several departments within the organization, including marketing, public relations, broadcasting, sales, advertising, ticket sales, community relations, and accounting. Since team presidents must develop strategies to encourage fans to attend games, it is good if they have some experience in public relations or marketing. Along with the public relations manager, team presidents create give-away programs, such as cap days or poster nights.

Another one of the team president's responsibilities is encouraging community relations by courting season ticket holders, as well as those who purchase luxury box seats, known as skyboxes. Usually, this involves selling these seats to corporations.

General managers handle the daily business activities of the teams, such as hiring and firing, promotions, supervising scouting, making trades, and negotiating player contracts. All sports teams have general managers, and usually the main functions of the job are the same regardless of the team's professional level. However, some general managers that work with minor league teams might also deal with additional job duties, including managing the souvenir booths or organizing the ticket offices. The most important asset the general manager brings to an organization is knowledge of business practices.

Sports executives for the NBA's Portland Trailblazers announce the drafting of Greg Oden (center), the number one pick in the National Basketball Association's amateur draft in 2007. *(Richard Clement, Reuters, Corbis)*

REQUIREMENTS

High School

High school courses that will help you to become a sports executive include business, mathematics, and computer science. English, speech, and physical education courses will also be beneficial. Managing a school club or other organization will give you a general idea of the responsibilities and demands that this career involves.

Postsecondary Training

To become a sports executive, you will need at least a bachelor's degree. Remember, even though this is a sport-related position, presidents and general managers are expected to have the same backgrounds as corporate executives. Most have master's degrees in sports administration, and some have master's degrees in business administration.

Other Requirements

Sports executives must create a positive image for their teams. In this age of extensive media coverage (including the frequent public speaking engagements that are required of sports executives), excellent communications skills are a must. Sports executives need to be dynamic public speakers. They also need a keen business sense and an intimate knowledge of how to forge a good relationship with their communities. They also should have excellent organizational skills, be detail oriented, and be sound decision-makers.

EXPLORING

One way to start exploring this field is to volunteer to do something for your school's sports teams, for example, chart statistics or take on the duties of equipment manager. This is a way to begin learning how athletic departments work. Talk to the general manager of your local minor league baseball club, and try to get a part-time job with the team during the summer. When you are in college, try to get an internship within the athletic department to supplement your course of study. Any experience you gain in any area of sports administration will be valuable to you in your career as a sports executive. You may also find it helpful to read publications such as *Sports Business Journal* (http://www.sportsbusinessjournal.com).

EMPLOYERS

Employers include professional, collegiate, and minor-league football, hockey, baseball, basketball, soccer, and other sports teams.

They are located across the United States and the world. About 9 percent of all athletes, coaches, and sports officials and related workers are employed in the commercial sports industry.

STARTING OUT

A majority of all sports executives begin their careers as interns. Interning offers the opportunity to gain recognition in an otherwise extremely competitive industry. Internships vary in length and generally include college credits. They are available in hundreds of sports categories and are offered by more than 90 percent of existing sports organizations. If you are serious about working in the sports industry, an internship is the most effective method of achieving your goals.

Entry-level positions in the sports industry are generally reserved for individuals with intern or volunteer experience. Once you have obtained this experience, you are eligible for thousands of entry-level positions in hundreds of fields. Qualified employees are hard to find in any industry, so the experience you have gained through internships will prove invaluable at this stage of your career.

ADVANCEMENT

The experience prerequisite to qualify for a management-level position is generally three to five years in a specific field within the sports industry. At this level, an applicant should have experience managing a small to medium-sized staff and possess specific skills, including marketing, public relations, broadcasting, sales, advertising, publications, sports medicine, licensing, and specific sport player development.

The minimum experience to qualify for an executive position is generally seven years. Executives with proven track records in the minors can be promoted to positions in the majors. Major league executives might receive promotions in the form of job offers from more prestigious teams.

EARNINGS

General managers, team presidents, and other sports executives earn salaries that range from $20,000 to $50,000 per year in the minor leagues to more than $1 million in the majors. Most sports executives are eligible for typical fringe benefits including medical and dental insurance, paid sick days and vacation time, and access to retirement savings plans.

WORK ENVIRONMENT

Sports team management is a fickle industry. When a team is winning, everyone loves the general manager or team president. When the team is losing, fans and the media often take out their frustrations on the team's executives. Sports executives must be able to handle that pressure. This industry is extremely competitive, and executives might find themselves without a job several times in their careers. Sports executives sleep, eat, and breathe their jobs and definitely love the sports they manage.

OUTLOOK

The U.S. Department of Labor predicts that employment in amusement and recreation services (a category that includes sports-related careers) will grow by about 25 percent through 2014, which is higher than the 14 percent growth predicted for all industries.

Although there are more sports executive positions available due to league expansion and the creation of new leagues, such as the Women's National Basketball Association, there still remain only a limited number of positions, and the competition for these jobs is very fierce. Being a sports executive demands both above-average business and leadership skills, in addition to a solid understanding of the demands and intricacies of a professional sports team. Those who obtain these jobs usually do so after many years of hard work. For that same reason, the rate of turnover in this field is low.

FOR MORE INFORMATION

Visit the society's Web site for information on membership for college students and a list of colleges and universities that offer sports management programs.
North American Society for Sport Management
Email: nassm@sru.edu
http://www.nassm.com

To learn more about sports executives, contact
Teamwork Online LLC
22550 McCauley Road
Shaker Heights, OH 44122-2718
Tel: 216-360-1790
Email: info@teamworkonline.com
http://www.teamworkonline.com

Sports Facility Designers

QUICK FACTS

School Subjects
Art
Mathematics

Personal Skills
Communication/ideas
Technical/scientific

Work Environment
Primarily indoors
One location with some
travel

Minimum Education Level
Bachelor's degree

Salary Range
$18,000 to $64,150 to
$125,000+

Certification or Licensing
Required

Outlook
About as fast as the average

DOT
001

GOE
02.07.03

NOC
2151

O*NET-SOC
17-1011.00

OVERVIEW

Sports facility designers are architects and engineers who specialize in the planning, design, and construction of facilities used for sporting and other public events. The buildings that these professionals design may be anything from a community gymnasium to a retractable domed stadium accommodating nearly 100,000 spectators. They consult with clients, plan layouts, prepare drawings of proposed buildings, write specifications, and prepare scale and full-sized drawings.

Sports facility designers also may help clients to obtain bids, select a contractor, and negotiate the construction contract, and they also visit construction sites to ensure that the work is being completed according to specification. Many sports facilities and convention centers are owned and financed by the municipality in which they are located; this means they have to go through a long approval and financing process before construction can begin. Throughout this process, the sports facility designer may be called upon to give his or her expert advice about questions and approve, or sign, the structural drawings.

HISTORY

Stadiums and arenas are structures that are specifically designed for sporting events, from football to figure skating to tennis. The name comes from the Greek word, *stade,* for a unit of measurement roughly equal to 606 feet—the length of the footrace in the ancient

Olympics and the overall length of the ancient Greek stadiums. The forum for the first Olympics, a stadium at Olympia, dates from the fourth century B.C.

In addition to stadiums, the Greeks built hippodromes for their chariot races. Wider than the horseshoe-shaped stadium used for all athletic events, the Greek hippodromes could accommodate several four-horse chariots racing alongside one another. Eventually, chariot racing became a featured part of athletic competitions, and the resulting structure was the Roman Circus. Rome's Circus Maximus was the finest example. Built in the first century B.C., historians believe it held as many as 250,000 spectators who viewed the spectacular feats from three sides. The Romans also built amphitheaters, impressive less for the vast numbers of spectators who could view each event (only 50,000 Romans could squeeze inside these vast areas) than for the fact that nothing obstructed their views. While the most famous of these structures is the Colosseum in Rome, now in ruins, the best preserved amphitheater is located in Arles, France, and is still being used for events, including the renowned summer music series, Les Choregies.

From ancient Greece to the present, however, the requirements of different sports have dictated the size, seating, and playing area of sports facilities. For example, a variety of shapes were originally used to construct stadiums for American-style football, from Harvard's U-shaped stadium (Cambridge, Massachusetts, 1912) to the facing crescent stands featured at Northwestern University (Evanston, Illinois, 1926). Innovations to these basic shapes weren't long in coming; the original Yankee stadium in New York, built in 1923, added seats protected by a roof. Dodger Stadium in Los Angeles, built in 1962, was the first tiered stadium without columns, and offered every fan an unobstructed view.

As stadiums and arenas began to be used for more than one sport or event, a trend toward multipurpose stadiums developed. Movable seating, first introduced in New York's Shea Stadium in 1964, allowed seats to be moved or rearranged according to the sport or expected crowd capacity. Specialty flooring allowed a stadium to be used for both hockey and basketball games.

The domed stadium, featuring internal climate control and artificial turf, was the next innovation, and this changed the face of many sports. Where playing times and broadcasts had previously relied on good weather and daylight, domed stadiums meant that play could continue in poor weather and at night.

Today's stadium or arena provides more than a playing field and seats for the spectators, however. The modern sports facility usually has one or more of the following: practice areas; home and visiting team locker rooms; physical therapy areas; sports equipment storage; press rooms; press boxes; facility maintenance equipment storage; cafeterias; food vendor areas; and offices for those who run the various aspects of the facility and teams who play there. The individuals who design these venues for sports events are responsible for making certain that the building functions to accommodate the varied events taking place there without sacrificing beauty or grace in structure. Today's stadiums are feats of engineering, combining structural integrity with space-age materials and engineering.

The field of modern sports facility design made a dramatic resurgence in the early 1980s. Prior to this time, no architectural firm existed that specialized in the design of sports facilities. Then, in 1983, four architects created HOK Sport, a division of Hellmuth, Obata, and Kassabaum Inc., the largest architectural firm in the United States. HOK Sport is now called HOK Sport+Venue+Event and is the leading sports facility design firm in the United States.

THE JOB

A sports facility designer normally has two responsibilities: to design a building that will satisfy the client (and the paying crowds) and protect the public's health, safety, and welfare. In order to accomplish these goals, facility designers must be licensed architects in the state in which they work. This means pursuing a difficult course of education, internships, apprenticeships, and examinations—all of which culminates in the architect receiving the proper credentials in the form of a license.

In order to create a design that is pleasing to client and fan alike, sports facility designers take on many roles. The job begins with learning what the client wants; that is, for what purpose is the stadium or arena or other sports facility being constructed? Will the facility house one team? Will it be a multipurpose or multiuse facility? What is the budget? Are there any special requests or requirements outside of those regulated by law? The answers to these questions inform the designer's approach to the project. Once these issues have been taken into consideration, the designer moves forward and begins to consider other, equally important issues, such as climate, water tables, zoning laws, fire regulation, local and state building regulations, the soil on which the building is to be constructed, the client's financial limitations, and many other requirements and regulations. The designer then prepares a set of plans that, upon the client's approval, will be developed into final design and construction documents. Many, many meetings take place in the interim, as the client's needs and requests are weighed against the legal issues involved. A certain amount of compromise generally occurs on the part of all the parties involved, although much less leeway comes from those parties representing the legal requirements.

The final design shows the exact dimensions of every portion of the building, including the location and size of columns and beams, electrical outlets and fixtures, plumbing, heating and air-conditioning facilities, seats and seating arrangements, doors, and all other features of the building.

The sports facility designer works closely with consulting engineers to design the plumbing, air conditioning, and electrical work. If the facility is to be used for concerts, an acoustical expert might be brought into the project. Lighting experts are consulted to select and place lighting fixtures and elements for evening or indoor performances.

The sports facility designer then will assist the client in getting bids from general contractors, one of which will be selected to construct the building to the specifications. The sports facility designer will assist the client through the completion of the construction and occupancy phases, making certain the correct materials are used and that the drawings and specifications are faithfully followed.

Throughout the process the sports facility designer works closely with a design or project team. This team is usually made up of the following: designers, who specialize in design development; a *structural designer,* who designs the frame of the building in accordance with the work of the sports facility designer; the *project manager* or *job superintendent,* who sees that the full detail drawings are completed to the satisfaction of the sports facility designer; and the *specification writer* and *estimator,* who prepare a project manual that describes in more detail the materials to be used in the building, their quality and method of installation, and all details related to the construction of the building.

The sports facility designer's job is very complex. He or she is expected to know construction methods, engineering principles and practices, and materials. The sports facility designer must also be up-to-date on new design and construction techniques and procedures.

REQUIREMENTS

High School

If you are hoping to enter the sports facility design profession, take a college-preparatory program that includes courses in English, mathematics, physics, art (especially freehand drawing), social studies, history, and foreign languages. Courses in business and computer science also will be useful.

Postsecondary Training

Most schools of architecture offer a five-year program leading to a bachelor of architecture degree or a six-year master of architecture program. In the six-year program, a preprofessional degree is awarded after four years, and the graduate degree after a two-year program. Many students prepare for an architectural career by first earning a liberal arts degree, then completing a three- to four-year master of architecture program.

A typical college architectural program includes courses in architectural history and theory, building design—including its technical and legal aspects—science, and liberal arts.

Certification or Licensing

All states and the District of Columbia require that individuals be licensed before calling themselves architects or contracting to provide sports facility design services in that particular state. The requirements for registration include graduation from an accredited school of architecture and three years of practical experience, or internship, in a licensed architect's office before the individual is eligible to take the rigorous Architect Registration Examination. Because most state architecture boards require a professional degree, high school students are advised, early in their senior year, to apply for admission to a professional program that is accredited by the National Architectural Accrediting Board (NAAB). Competition to enter these programs is high. Grades, class rank, and aptitude and achievement scores play a very large part in determining who will be accepted.

Other Requirements

To be successful in this career, you should be well prepared academically and be intelligent, observant, responsible, and self-disciplined. You should have a concern for detail and accuracy, be able to communicate effectively both orally and in writing, and be able to accept criticism constructively.

Although great artistic ability is not necessary, you should be able to visualize spatial relationships and have the capacity to solve technical problems. Mathematical ability is also important. In addition, you should possess organizational skills and leadership qualities and be able to work well with others.

Largest Stadiums in the World by Capacity

Name	Location	Capacity
1. Indianapolis Speedway	Indianapolis, Ind., United States	250,000
2. Tokyo Racecourse	Tokyo, Japan	223,000
3. Shanghai International Circuit	Shanghai, China	200,000
4. Daytona International Speedway	Daytona Beach, Fla., United States	168,000
5. Lowe's Motor Speedway	Charlotte, N.C., United States	167,000
6. Nakayama Racecourse	Chiba, Japan	165,676
7. Bristol Motor Speedway	Bristol, Tenn., United States	160,000
8. Istanbul Park	Istanbul, Turkey	155,000
9. Texas Motor Speedway	Fort Worth, Tex., United States	154,861
10. Rungrado May Day Stadium	Pyongyang, North Korea	150,000
10. Nürburgring	Nürburgring, Germany	150,000
12. Talladega Superspeedway	Talladega, Ala., United States	143,000
13. Circuit de Catalunya	Montmeló, Spain	140,700
14. Dover International Speedway	Dover, Del., United States	140,000
14. Las Vegas Motor Speedway	Las Vegas, Nev., United States	140,000
16. Hanshin Racecourse	Hyogo, Japan	139,877
17. Autodromo di Monza	Monza, Italy	137,000
18. Michigan International Speedway	Brooklyn, Mich., United States	136,373
19. Rockingham Speedway	Corby, Great Britain	130,000
19. Flemington Racecourse	Melbourne, Australia	130,000

Source: Worldstadiums.com

EXPLORING

Most sports facility designers will welcome the opportunity to talk with you about entering the field and may be willing to let you visit their offices where you can gain a first hand knowledge of the type of work done by sports facility designers.

Other opportunities may include visiting the design studios of a school of architecture or working for an architect or building contractor during summer vacations. Also, many architecture schools offer summer programs for high school students. Books and magazines on architecture and sports facility design provide a broad understanding of the nature of the work and the values of the profession.

EMPLOYERS

There are approximately 129,000 registered architects employed in the United States. Certainly there are not nearly this number of sports facility designers, as this is a specialized discipline within the field of architecture. Most sports facility designers work in architectural firms. Others work in allied fields, such as construction, engineering, interior design, landscape architecture, or real estate development.

While many design firms handle small community projects, the large stadiums, civic centers, arenas, ballparks, and other sports facilities are almost exclusively handled by one firm, the firm that practically created the field of facility design, HOK Sport+Venue+Event, based in Kansas City, Missouri.

Most designers who work in this fieldwork for HOK Sport+Venue+Event because this division of the nation's largest architectural firm receives 95 percent of the major sports facility design commissions in the world. As the world's preeminent sports architecture design firm, HOK Sport+Venue+Event has developed a diverse portfolio of arena and stadium projects worldwide for public sector clients, professional sports franchises, and colleges and universities.

STARTING OUT

Those entering sports facility design following graduation start as interns in an architectural firm that specializes in sports facility design. As an intern, you will assist in preparing architectural documents. You will also handle related details, such as administering contracts, coordinating the work of other professionals on the project, researching building codes and construction materials, and writing specifications.

As an alternative to working for an architectural firm, some architecture graduates go into allied fields such as construction, engineering, interior design, landscape architecture, or real estate development. Others may develop graphic, interior design, or product specialties. Still others put their training to work in the theater, film, or television fields or in museums, display firms, and architectural product and materials manufacturing companies. No matter where you serve your internship, it usually always adds to your perception of space, materials, and techniques. However, if you wish to focus on the field of sports facility design, you should try to find internships with architectural or engineering firms that have worked on stadium, arena, or other facility projects in the past.

ADVANCEMENT

Interns and architects alike are given progressively more complex jobs. Sports facility designers may advance to supervisory or managerial positions. Some sports facility designers become partners in established firms, but the eventual goal of many designers is to establish their own practice.

EARNINGS

Beginning intern architects earn salaries ranging from $18,000 to $27,000 annually, according to the Association of Collegiate Schools of Architecture. Median annual earnings for architects were $64,150 in 2006, according to the U.S. Department of Labor. Salaries ranged from less than $39,420 to $104,970 or more annually.

Well-established sports facility designers who are partners in an architectural firm or who have their own businesses generally earn much more than do the salaried employees. Those who are partners in very large firms can earn more than $125,000 a year. Most employers offer such fringe benefits as health insurance, sick and vacation pay, and retirement plans.

WORK ENVIRONMENT

Sports facility designers normally work a 40-hour week with their hours falling between 8 A.M. and 6 P.M. There may be times when they will have to work overtime, especially when under pressure to complete an assignment.

Sports facility designers usually work in comfortable offices, but they may spend a considerable amount of time outside of the office, visiting clients or viewing the progress of a particular job in the field. Their routines usually vary considerably, which means they may go from the office to a hard-hat construction site to a materials plant to a swanky lunch and then back to the office until late into the evening.

OUTLOOK

As urban centers struggle to compete for tourism and convention business, the presence of a popular sports franchise becomes increasingly important. In order to lure large franchises within the major sports of baseball, basketball, football, and hockey, cities have gone to great lengths, the most successful of which has been the construction of modern sports facilities. The boom in sports facility construction is far from over, but it might begin to show signs of slowing down in the next several years.

Employment in the field is expected to grow about as fast as average for all occupations over the next several years. The number of sports facility designers needed will depend on the volume of construction, but with more and more local municipalities constructing sports stadiums and convention centers in an effort to stimulate the local economy, the outlook is favorable. The construction industry is extremely sensitive to fluctuation in the overall economy, and a recession could result in layoffs.

On the positive side, employment of sports facility designers is not likely to be affected by the growing use of computer technologies. Rather than replacing sports facility designers, computers are being used to enhance the sports facility designer's work.

Competition for employment will continue to be strong, particularly for positions with HOK Sport+Venue+Event. Openings will not be newly created positions but will become available as otherwise established architects transfer to other employers or leave the field.

FOR MORE INFORMATION

For career and scholarship information and a list of NAAB-accredited programs in architecture, contact
American Institute of Architects
1735 New York Avenue, NW
Washington, DC 20006-5209
Tel: 800-242-3837

Email: infocentral@aia.org
http://www.aia.org

For information on architectural schools, contact
Association of Collegiate Schools of Architecture
1735 New York Avenue, NW
Washington, DC 20006-5209
Tel: 202-785-2324
Email: info@acsa-arch.org
http://www.acsa-arch.org

HOK Sport+Venue+Event is the main employer of sports facility designers. Contact them for employment information:
HOK Sport+Venue+Event
323 West 8th Street, Suite 700
Kansas City, MO 64105
Tel: 816-221-1500
Email: sport@hok.com
http://www.hoksve.com

For information on accredited architectural training programs, contact
National Architectural Accrediting Board
1735 New York Avenue, NW
Washington, DC 20006-5209
Tel: 202-783-2007
Email: info@naab.org
http://www.naab.org

For information on its Intern Development Program, the Architect Registration Examination, and certification and continuing education, contact
National Council of Architectural Registration Boards
1801 K Street, NW, Suite 1100-K
Washington, DC 20006-1310
Tel: 202-783-6500
http://www.ncarb.org

Sports Facility Managers

OVERVIEW

Stadium, *arena*, and *facility managers*, sometimes called *general managers*, *sports facility managers*, or *stadium operations executives*, are responsible for the day-to-day operations involved in running a sports facility. They are involved in sports facility planning, including the buying, selling, or leasing of facilities; facility redesign and construction; and the supervision of sports facilities, including the structures and grounds, as well as the custodial crews.

HISTORY

Today's stadiums or arenas provide much more than a playing field and seats for sports and event spectators. The modern sports facility usually has one or more of the following: practice areas, home and visiting team locker rooms, physical therapy areas, sports equipment storage, press rooms, press boxes, facility maintenance equipment storage, cafeterias, food vendor areas, and offices for those who run the various aspects of the facility and teams who play there, as well as promote and market both facility and team. Those who manage these venues for sports events are responsible for ensuring that everything runs smoothly for the athletes, the fans, the advertisers, the media, and their own staff.

THE JOB

Stadium, arena, and facility managers are responsible for the day-to-day operations involved in running a sports facility. In the simplest terms, the manager of a sports facility, like other facility managers, must coordinate the events that occur in the facility with the services and people who make those events possible.

Sports facility managers are involved in sports facility planning, including the buying, selling, or leasing of facilities; facility redesign and construction; and the supervision of sports facilities, including the structures and grounds, as well as the custodial crews. This may mean months, sometimes even years, of research and long-term planning. Crucial resources and issues the manager might investigate include: sports facility design firms; prospective sites for the new facility and analyses of neighborhood support for a facility; and zoning laws or other federal, state, and local regulations concerning the construction of new buildings. Politics can play a key part in this process; the manager might be involved in these political meetings, as well. Once ground is broken on the new site, a sports facility manager may then divide his or her time between the construction site and the existing site, supervising both facilities until the new one is completed.

The manager of a sports facility, stadium, or arena who is not involved in the construction of a new facility, or the redesign of an existing one, spends most of his or her time in the office or somewhere in the facility itself, supervising the day-to-day management of the facility. The manager usually determines the organizational structure of the facility and establishes the personnel staffing requirements; setting up the manner in which things will be done and by whom. The facility manager is constantly analyzing how many different workers are needed to run the various areas of the facility efficiently, without sacrificing quality. The manager addresses staffing needs as they arise, setting the education, experience, and performance standards for each position. Depending on the size of the facility and the nature of the manager's assigned responsibilities, this may mean hiring a personnel director to screen prospective employees, or it may mean the manager personally sifts through stacks of resumes whenever a position opens up. Usually, all policies and procedures having to do with the morale, safety, service, appearance, and performance of facility employees (and which are not determined by the organization, itself) are determined by the manager.

The manager of a sports facility is also responsible for assisting with the development and coordination of the facility's annual operating calendar, including activity schedules, dates and hours of operation, and projections for attendance and revenue. Often, a manager for a sports facility directs and assists with the procurement of activities and events to take place at the facility; this, of course, depends on the size of the facility. A large, multipurpose stadium, for example, will probably have at least one individual devoted to event planning and the acquisition of activities. Even in this case, however, the sports facility manager must be involved in coordinating the event with all the other aspects of the facility.

The sports facility manager handles the negotiations, contracts, and agreements with industry agents, suppliers, and vendors. These days, many jobs that used to be handled in-house by staff employees are now contracted out to private companies that specialize in that aspect of the event. Food service and security, for example, are two areas that are usually privately managed by outside vendors and firms. It is the responsibility of the sports facility manager to hire such contractors and to monitor the quality of their work.

Finally, it is the manager's duty to make certain that the facility, its workers, and the services it offers are in accordance with federal, state, and local regulations.

Although certain responsibilities are shared, the job description for a sports facility manager will inevitably vary according to the type of sport played and the level of the organization that employs the manager. For example, the duties of a manager for a parks and recreation facility in a medium-sized town will differ considerably from those of the general manager of Churchill Downs in Louisville, Kentucky; the former will do many of the duties that the latter would most likely delegate to others.

The type of sports stadium, arena, or auditorium in which sports facility managers work also varies, from race tracks to natatoriums to large, multipurpose stadiums that host football games and rock concerts.

REQUIREMENTS

High School
High school courses that will give you a general background for work in sports facility management include business, mathematics, government, and computer science. Speech and writing classes will help you to hone your communication skills. Managing a school club or other organization will give you an introduction to overseeing budgets and the work of others.

Postsecondary Training
These days, a bachelor's degree is pretty much required to enter the field of sports facility management. Although in the past it wasn't necessary, the competition for jobs in sports administration and facility management is so keen that a bachelor's degree is nearly

mandatory. In fact, in many instances, a master's degree in sports administration or sports facility management is increasingly required of managers.

The oldest program in the country in sports administration and facility management is at Ohio University in Athens, Ohio. Administered by the School of Recreation and Sports Sciences within Ohio University's College of Health and Human Services, the program requires 55 credit hours (five of which are completed during an internship) and leads to the master of sports administration degree. The curriculum focuses on business administration, journalism, communications, management, marketing, sports administration, and facility management. The required internship lasts anywhere from three months to a year and internship opportunities are provided by more than 400 different organizations worldwide. (See "For More Information" at the end of this article for contact information for this program.)

Certification or Licensing

At the moment, certification in facility management is not mandatory, but it is becoming a distinguishing credential among the managers of the largest, most profitable venues. A sports stadium or arena brings its owners a lot of revenue, and these owners aren't willing to trust the management of such lucrative venues to individuals who are not qualified to run them; certification is one way an administration can ensure that certain industry standards in facility management are met. The International Facility Management Association, probably the industry leader in certification, offers the designation of certified facility manager. The International Association of Assembly Managers also offers the certification designation of certified facilities executive. For contact information for these associations, see the end of this article.

Other Requirements

Most organizations want their facility managers to have, at a minimum, five years of experience in the field or industry. This may include participation in a sport at the professional level, marketing or promotions work, or related management experience that can be shown as relevant to the responsibilities and duties of a sports facility manager.

Leadership and communication skills are considered essential to be successful in this career. In the course of an average day, you might review designs for a new stadium with top-level executives, release a statement to members of the press about the

It Takes More Than Athletes to Make a Sporting Event a Success

The Wimbledon Championships, which are held in Great Britain each summer, are considered by many to be the "holy grail" of professional tennis competition. Started in 1877, the Championships were initially watched by only a few hundred spectators. Today, nearly 500,000 spectators—as well as those who enjoy the competition via television, radio, and the Internet—watch tennis superstars such as Roger Federer, Venus and Serena Williams, Rafael Nadal, and other athletes from more than 60 countries compete for prizes. While the athletes are the ultimate draw, it takes a wide variety of workers to make a sporting event a success. According to Wimbledon.org, the following workers are needed each year to keep the Wimbledon Championships running smoothly:

Ball Boys and Ball Girls: 290
Ball Distributors: 7
Carpenters, Electricians, and Other Trades Workers: 6
Catering Workers: 1,600
Court Attendants: 128
Court Officials: 335
Dressing Room Attendants: 18
Electronic Scoreboard Operators and Data Collectors: 46
Ground Cleaners: 75
Grounds and Maintenance Workers: 46
Honorary Stewards: 150
Left Luggage Attendants: 30
Lift Operators: 30
Office Cleaners: 75
Physiotherapists: 13
Practice Court Attendants: 6
Press Staff: 18
Referee's Office: 16
Security Guards: 480
Service and London Fire Brigade Stewards: 490
Speed of Service Operators: 8
Transport Service Drivers: 310
Washroom Attendants: 112
Web Professionals: 15

Source: Wimbledon.org

groundbreaking ceremony for the new stadium, and interview prospective foremen for maintenance work. You will need to be able to state clearly and concisely your ideas, information, and goals, regardless of the audience.

Finally, you should possess excellent strategic, budgetary, and operational planning skills; the day-to-day operations of the sports facility will run on the decisions that you make, so you need to be capable of juggling many different tasks.

EXPLORING

If you aren't actively involved with a sport as a participant, you can get involved with sports administration and management by volunteering for positions with your own high school teams. All experience helps, beginning with organizing and managing the equipment for a football team, for example, all the way up to working as a team statistician. You can also work with their local booster club to sponsor events that promote athletics within the school district. These activities demonstrate your interest and devotion and may help you in the future by providing you with an edge when searching for an internship.

Part-time or summer jobs as ushers, vendors, ball boys or girls, for example, not only provide firsthand experience for both high school and college students, but can lead to other contacts and opportunities.

College students interested in sports facility management can often locate valuable internships through contacts they have developed from part-time jobs, but the placement centers in undergraduate or graduate programs in business administration and facility management are also good places to consult for information on internships. The professional leagues and associations for specific sports. The National Hockey League, the National Football League, and the National Basketball Association, for example, all offer summer internships. Competition for positions with these organizations is extremely keen, so interested students should send for application materials well in advance, study them, and apply early.

Professional organizations within the field also sponsor opportunities to learn on the job. The International Association of Assembly Managers (IAAM) offers internships to qualified students. Typically, participating facilities that serve as sites for IAAM internships are responsible for the selection of their interns. While some of these facilities aren't specifically geared toward sporting events, much of the management skills and responsibilities are shared and will provide you with a wonderful opportunity to learn firsthand.

EMPLOYERS

Sports facility managers may work for single team, a multisports arena or stadium, or they may work for a city or state organization, such as a parks and recreation department.

STARTING OUT

Graduates of programs in sports administration and sports facility management usually find jobs through internships they have had, personal contacts they developed in the field, or from job listings in their graduate programs' placement departments.

Entry-level jobs may be in facility management, or they may come in a related field. Most organizations like to promote from within, so it isn't uncommon for someone with a bachelor's or graduate degree in facility management who is working in, for example, public relations, to be considered first for an opening in the sports facility department. Associate- or assistant-level positions are the most likely entry point for graduates, but those with exceptional education and experience may qualify for managerial positions after graduation, although this is rare. In fact, as the field becomes more popular, it will be increasingly difficult to enter a sports facility management position without a bachelor's degree and a solid internship experience, at the very least.

Those who find entry-level jobs are helped by mentors. Mentoring is an industry-supported method in which an older, experienced member of a facility management team helps a younger, less-experienced individual to learn the ropes. This process helps the person learn and aids the organization by reducing problems caused by inexperienced beginners.

ADVANCEMENT

Experience and certification are the best ways for someone to advance in this field. Years of successful on-the-job experience count for a great deal in this industry; the owners and administrations of professional teams and sports venues look for someone who has demonstrated the ability to make things run smoothly. Certification is becoming another way in which success can be gauged; more and more frequently, certification garners salary increases and promotions for those who hold it. Increasingly, firms are asking for certified facility managers when they begin job searches. Since certification goes hand-in-hand with experience, it is assumed that certified individuals are the best in their field.

Outside of experience and certification, a willingness and eagerness to learn and branch into new areas is a less objective manner for gauging which managers will land top jobs. Those who are willing to embrace new technology and are open to new ideas and methods for improving efficiency will very likely advance in their careers.

Advancement might also mean changing specialties or developing one. Sports facility managers who are interested in other areas of management may decide to leave the field and involve themselves with different venues, such as auditoriums, performing arts centers, or convention centers, to name just a few. Still others might advance to manage international venues.

EARNINGS

Earnings for sports facility managers vary considerably depending on their experience and education, as well as the level of the facility that employs them. Administrative services managers (the category under which the U.S. Department of Labor classifies sports facility managers) earned median annual salaries of $67,690 in 2006. The lowest paid 10 percent earned less than $34,970, and the highest paid 10 percent earned $117,610 or more per year. Facility managers who are certified earn higher salaries than those who are not certified. The International Facility Management Association reports that members who held the certified facility manager designation earned an average 13 percent more than their non-certified counterparts.

WORK ENVIRONMENT

One of the perks of the profession is the glamorous atmosphere that the job promotes; sports facility managers work to provide a unique environment for amateur and professional athletes, sometimes even celebrities and other performers. Although their work most often is behind-the-scenes, they may have indirect or direct contact with the high-profile personalities who perform in large venues. Sports facility managers usually work in clean, comfortable offices. Since their work often involves other activities, such as construction, they also may spend a great deal of time at construction sites and in trailers, supervising the construction of a new facility.

The management of a sports arena or stadium naturally involves promotional events, both for the building and the teams or events that are staged there. To be successful in their work, facility managers must maintain regular contact with the members of other departments, such as marketing and public relations.

A sports facility manager's job can be stressful. Construction, renovation, and cleaning and maintenance deadlines must all be met in order to ensure the efficient operation of a sports facility, let alone one in which major sports events occur. Depending on the level of the facility and the nature of events that are staged there, the responsibilities of the manager often require more hours on the job than the typical nine-to-five day allows. Additional work may be necessary, but is often uncompensated.

OUTLOOK

In general, the future for facilities managers is much brighter than it is for those in other administrative services. This relatively young field is growing quickly and, especially in the private sector, is not as subject to cost-cutting pressures or as vulnerable to government cutbacks. Demand for jobs in sports administration is great, and the newer field of sports facility management is quickly catching up.

FOR MORE INFORMATION

For certification information, job listings, student chapters, internships, and to subscribe to Facility Manager, *contact*
International Association of Assembly Managers
635 Fritz Drive, Suite 100
Coppell, TX 75019-4442
Tel: 972-906-7441
http://www.iaam.org

For information on certification and to subscribe to Facility Management Journal, *contact*
International Facility Management Association
1 East Greenway Plaza, Suite 1100
Houston, TX 77046-0194
Tel: 713-623-4362
Email: ifmahq@ifma.org
http://www.ifma.org

For information on the master of sports administration degree, contact
Sports Administration/Facility Management Program
Ohio University
School of Recreation and Sport Sciences
RTEC 218

Athens, OH 45701-2979
Tel: 740-593-4666
Email: sportsad@ohiou.edu
http://www.cats.ohiou.edu/sportadmin

For industry information, contact
Stadium Managers Association
525 SW 5th Street, Suite A
Des Moines, IA 50309-4501
Tel: 515-282-8192
http://www.stadiummanagers.org

Sports Instructors and Coaches

QUICK FACTS

School Subjects
English
Physical education

Personal Skills
Communication/ideas
Helping/teaching

Work Environment
Indoors and outdoors
Primarily multiple locations

Minimum Education Level
Some postsecondary training

Salary Range
$13,990 to $26,950 to
$5,000,000+

Certification or Licensing
Required in certain positions

Outlook
Faster than the average

DOT
153

GOE
01.10.01

NOC
5252

O*NET-SOC
27-2022.00

OVERVIEW

Sports instructors demonstrate and explain the skills and rules of particular sports, like golf or tennis, to individuals or groups. They help beginners learn basic rules, stances, grips, movements, and techniques of a game. Sports instructors often help experienced athletes to sharpen their skills.

Coaches work with a single, organized team or individual, teaching the skills associated with that sport. A coach prepares her or his team for competition. During the competition, he or she continues to give instruction from a vantage point near the court or playing field.

HISTORY

Americans have more leisure time than ever and many have decided that they are going to put this time to good use by getting or staying in shape. This fitness boom, as well as a trend toward more sports competitions, has created employment opportunities for many sports-related occupations.

Health clubs, community centers, parks and recreational facilities, and private business now employ sports instructors who teach everything from tennis and golf to scuba diving.

As high school and college sports become even more organized, there continues to be a need for coaches qualified to teach the intricate skills associated with athletics today.

THE JOB

The specific job requirements of sports instructors and coaches vary according to the type of sport and athletes involved. For example, an instructor teaching advanced skiing at a resort in Utah will have different duties and responsibilities than an instructor teaching beginning swimming at a municipal pool. Nevertheless, all instructors and coaches are teachers. They must be very knowledgeable about rules and strategies for their respective sports. They must also have an effective teaching method that reinforces correct techniques and procedures so their students or players will be able to gain from that valuable knowledge. Also, instructors and coaches need to be aware of and open to new procedures and techniques. Many attend clinics or seminars to learn more about their sport or even how to teach more effectively. Many are also members of professional organizations that deal exclusively with their sport.

Safety is a primary concern for all coaches and instructors. Coaches and instructors make sure their students have the right equipment and know its correct use. A major component of safety is helping students feel comfortable and confident with their abilities. This entails teaching the proper stances, techniques, and movements of a game, instructing students on basic rules, and answering any questions.

While instructors may tutor students individually or in small groups, a coach works with all the members of a team. Both use lectures and demonstrations to show students the proper skills, and both point out students' mistakes or deficiencies.

Motivation is another key element in sports instruction. Almost all sports require stamina, and most coaches will tell you that psychological preparation is every bit as important as physical training.

Coaches and instructors also have administrative responsibilities. College coaches actively recruit new players to join their team. Professional coaches attend team meetings with owners and general managers to determine which players they will draft the next season. Sports instructors at health and athletic clubs schedule classes, lessons, and contests.

REQUIREMENTS

Training and educational requirements vary, depending on the specific sport and the ability level of students being instructed. Most coaches associated with schools have bachelor's degrees. Many middle and high school coaches are also teachers within the school. Most instructors need to combine several years of successful experience in a particular sport with some educational background, preferably in teaching. A college degree is becoming more important as part of an instructor's background.

High School
To prepare for college courses, high school students should take courses that teach human physiology. Biology, health, and exercise classes would all be helpful. Courses in English and speech are also important to improve or develop communication skills.

There is no substitute for developing expertise in a sport. If you can play the sport well and effectively explain to other people how they might play, you will most likely be able to get a job as a sports instructor. The most significant source of training for this occupation is gained while on the job.

Postsecondary Training
Postsecondary training in this field varies greatly. College and professional coaches often attended college as athletes, while others attended college and received their degrees without playing a sport. If you are interested in becoming a high school coach, you will need a college degree because you will most likely be teaching as well as coaching. At the high school level, coaches spend their days teaching everything from physical education to English to mathematics, and so the college courses these coaches take vary greatly. Coaches of some youth league sports may not need a postsecondary degree, but they must have a solid understanding of their sport and of injury prevention.

Certification or Licensing
Many facilities require sports instructors to be certified. Information on certification is available from any organization that deals with the specific sport in which one might be interested.

Since most high school coaches also work as teachers, those interested in this job should plan to obtain teacher certification in their state.

Other Requirements
Coaches have to be experts in their sport. They must have complete knowledge of the rules and strategies of the game, so that they can creatively design effective plays and techniques for their athletes. But the requirements for this job do not end here. Good coaches are able to communicate their extensive knowledge to the athletes in a way that not only instructs the athletes, but also inspires them to perform to their fullest potential. Therefore, coaches are also teachers.

Sports Coaches and Scouts: Earnings by Specialty, 2006

Industry	Mean Annual Earnings
Spectator sports	$60,150
Colleges, universities, and professional schools	$44,200
Other amusement and recreation industries	$32,890
Other schools of instruction	$28,040
Elementary and secondary schools	$27,550
Civic and social organizations	$25,120

Source: U.S. Department of Labor

"I think I'm good at my job because I love working with people and because I'm disciplined in everything I do," says Dawn Shannahan, former assistant girls' basketball and track coach at Leyden High School in Franklin Park, Illinois. Discipline is important for athletes, as they must practice plays and techniques over and over again. Coaches who cannot demonstrate and encourage this type of discipline will have difficulty helping their athletes improve. Shannahan adds, "I've seen coaches who are really knowledgeable about their sport but who aren't patient enough to allow for mistakes or for learning." Patience can make all the difference between an effective coach and one who is unsuccessful.

Similarly, Shannahan says, "A coach shouldn't be a pessimist. The team could be losing by a lot, but you have to stay optimistic and encourage the players." Coaches must be able to work under pressure, guiding teams through games and tournaments that carry great personal and possibly financial stakes for everyone involved.

EXPLORING

Try to gain as much experience as possible in all sports and a specific sport in particular. It is never too early to start. High school and college offer great opportunities to participate in sporting events as a player, manager, trainer, or in intramural leagues.

Most communities have sports programs such as Little League baseball or track and field meets sponsored by a recreation commission. Get involved by volunteering as a coach, umpire, or starter.

A coach discusses strategy with his junior league flag football team.
(Bob Daemmrich, The Image Works)

Talking with sports instructors already working in the field is also a good way to discover specific job information and find out about career opportunities.

EMPLOYERS

Besides working in high schools, coaches are hired by colleges and universities, professional sports teams, individual athletes such as tennis players, and by youth leagues, summer camps, and recreation centers.

STARTING OUT

People with expertise in a particular sport, who are interested in becoming an instructor, should apply directly to the appropriate facility. Sometimes a facility will provide training.

For those interested in coaching, many colleges offer positions to *graduate assistant coaches*. Graduate assistant coaches are recently graduated players who are interested in becoming coaches. They receive a stipend and gain valuable coaching experience.

ADVANCEMENT

Advancement opportunities for both instructors and coaches depend on the individual's skills, willingness to learn, and work ethic. A sports instructor's success can be measured by their students' caliber of play and the number of students they instruct. Successful instructors may become well known enough to open their own schools or camps, write books, or produce how-to videos.

Some would argue that a high percentage of wins is the only criteria for success for professional coaches. However, coaches in the scholastic ranks have other responsibilities and other factors that measure success; for example, high school and college coaches must make sure their players are getting good grades. All coaches must try to produce a team that competes in a sportsmanlike fashion regardless of whether they win or lose.

Successful coaches are often hired by larger schools. High school coaches may advance to become college coaches, and the most successful college coaches often are given the opportunity to coach professional teams. Former players sometimes land assistant or head coaching positions.

EARNINGS

Earnings for sports instructors and coaches vary considerably depending on the sport and the person or team being coached. The coach of a Wimbledon champion commands much more money per hour than the swimming instructor for the tadpole class at the municipal pool.

The U.S. Department of Labor reports that the median earnings for sports coaches and instructors were $26,950 in 2006. The lowest 10 percent earned less than $13,990, while the highest 10 percent earned more than $58,890. Sports instructors and coaches who worked at colleges and universities earned a mean annual salary of $44,200 in 2006, while those employed by elementary and secondary schools earned $27,550.

Much of the work is part time, and part-time employees generally do not receive paid vacations, sick days, or health insurance. Instructors who teach group classes for beginners through park districts or at city recreation centers can expect to earn around $6 per hour. An hour-long individual lesson through a golf course or tennis club averages $75. Many times, coaches for children's teams work as volunteers.

Many sports instructors work in camps teaching swimming, archery, sailing and other activities. These instructors generally earn between $1,000 and $2,500, plus room and board, for a summer session.

Full-time fitness instructors at gyms or health clubs earned salaries that ranged from less than $14,880 to $56,750 or more per year in 2006, with a median salary of $25,910, according to the U.S. Department of Labor. Instructors with many years of experience and a college degree have the highest earning potential.

Most coaches who work at the high school level or below also teach within the school district. Besides their teaching salary and coaching fee—either a flat rate or a percentage of their annual salary—school coaches receive a benefits package that includes paid vacations and health insurance.

Head college football coaches at NCAA Division I schools earned an average salary of $950,000 a year in 2006, according to *USA Today*. A few top football coaches earn more than $2 million annually. Some top coaches in men's Division I basketball earn salaries of $1 million or more, according to *USA Today*. Women's basketball coaches at the college level typically earn lower salaries than their colleagues who coach men's sports—although top coaches earn salaries that are on par with coaches of men's basketball teams.

Coaches for professional teams often earn between $200,000 and $3 million. Some top coaches can earn more than $5 million annually. Many popular coaches augment their salaries with fees from personal appearances and endorsements.

WORK ENVIRONMENT

An instructor or coach may work indoors, in a gym or health club, or outdoors, perhaps at a swimming pool. Much of the work is part time. Full-time sports instructors generally work between 35 and 40 hours per week. During the season when their teams compete, coaches can work 16 hours each day, five or six days each week.

It is not unusual for coaches or instructors to work evenings or weekends. Instructors work then because that is when their adult students are available for instruction. Coaches work nights and weekends because those are the times their teams compete.

One significant drawback to this job is the lack of job security. A club may hire a new instructor on very little notice, or may cancel a scheduled class for lack of interest. Athletic teams routinely fire coaches after losing seasons.

Sports instructors and coaches should enjoy working with a wide variety of people. They should be able to communicate clearly and possess good leadership skills to effectively teach complex skills. They can take pride in the knowledge that they have helped their students or their players reach new heights of achievement and training.

OUTLOOK

Americans' interest in health, physical fitness, and body image continues to send people to gyms and playing fields. This fitness boom has created strong employment opportunities for many people in sports-related occupations.

Health clubs, community centers, parks and recreational facilities, and private business now employ sports instructors who teach everything from tennis and golf to scuba diving.

According to the U.S. Department of Labor, these careers will grow faster than the average for all occupations through 2014. Job opportunities will be best in high schools and in amateur athletic leagues. Health clubs, adult education programs, and private industry will require competent, dedicated instructors. Those with the most training, education, and experience will have the best chance for employment.

The creation of new professional leagues, as well as the expansion of current leagues, will open some new employment opportunities for professional coaches, but competition for these jobs will be very intense. There will also be openings as other coaches retire, or are terminated. However, there is very little job security in coaching, unless a coach can consistently produce a winning team.

FOR MORE INFORMATION

For certification information, trade journals, job listings, and a list of graduate schools, visit the AAHPERD Web site.

American Alliance for Health, Physical Education, Recreation and Dance (AAHPERD)
1900 Association Drive
Reston, VA 20191-1598
Tel: 800-213-7193
http://www.aahperd.org

For information on membership and baseball coaching education, coaching Web links, and job listings, visit the ABCA Web site.

American Baseball Coaches Association (ABCA)
108 South University Avenue, Suite 3
Mount Pleasant, MI 48858-2327
Tel: 989-775-3300
Email: abca@abca.org
http://www.abca.org

For information on football coaching careers, contact
American Football Coaches Association
100 Legends Lane
Waco, TX 76706-1243
Tel: 254-754-9900
Email: info@afca.com
http://www.afca.com

To learn more about coaching hockey, contact
American Hockey Coaches Association
7 Concord Street
Gloucester, MA 01930-2300
Tel: 781-245-4177
http://www.ahcahockey.com

For information on careers in sports and physical education, contact
National Association for Sport and Physical Education
1900 Association Drive
Reston, VA 20191-1598
Tel: 800-213-7193
Email: naspe@aahperd.org
http://www.aahperd.org/naspe

For information on basketball coaching, contact
National Association of Basketball Coaches
1111 Main Street, Suite 1000
Kansas City, MO 64105-2136
Tel: 816-878-6222
http://nabc.ocsn.com

For information on high school coaching opportunities, contact
National High School Athletic Coaches Association
PO Box 10065
Fargo, ND 58106-0065
Email: office@hscoaches.org
http://www.hscoaches.org

To learn more about coaching soccer, contact
National Soccer Coaches Association of America
800 Ann Avenue
Kansas City, KS 66101-3003
Tel: 800-458-0678
http://www.nscaa.com

For information on women's basketball coaching, contact
Women's Basketball Coaches Association
4646 Lawrenceville Highway
Lilburn, GA 30047-3620
Tel: 770-279-8027
Email: wbca@wbca.org
http://www.wbca.org

Sports Physicians

OVERVIEW

Sports physicians, also known as *team physicians*, treat patients who have sustained injuries to their musculoskeletal systems during the play or practice of an individual or team sporting event. Sports physicians also do preparticipation tests and physical exams. Some sports physicians create educational programs to help athletes prevent injury. Sports physicians work for schools, universities, hospitals, and private offices; some also travel and treat members of professional sports teams.

HISTORY

The field of sports medicine, and nearly all the careers related to it, owes its foundation to experiments and studies conducted by Aristotle, Leonardo da Vinci, and Etienne Jules Marey. Aristotle's treatise on the gaits of humans and animals established the beginning of biomechanics. In one experiment, he used the sun as a transducer to illustrate how a person, when walking in a straight line, actually throws a shadow that produces not a correspondingly straight line, but a zigzag line. Leonardo da Vinci's forays into the range and type of human motion explored a number of questions, including grade locomotion, wind resistance on the body, the projection of the center of gravity onto a base of support, and stepping and standing studies.

However it was Marey, a French physiologist, who created much more advanced devices to study human motion. In fact, sports medicine and modern cinematography both claim him as the father of their respective fields. Marey built the first force platform, a device that was able to visualize the forces between the foot and the floor. Californian photographer Eadweard Muybridge's serial photographs of a horse in motion inspired Marey's invention of the chronophotograph. In contrast to Muybridge's consecutive frames, taken by several cameras, Marey's pictures with the chronophotograph superimposed the stages of action onto a single photograph; in essence, giving form to motion. By 1892, Marey had made primitive motion pictures, but his efforts were quickly eclipsed by those of film pioneers Louis and Auguste Lumiere.

Following both World Wars I and II, Marey's and others scientists' experiments with motion would combine with medicine's need to heal and/or completely replace the limbs of war veterans. To provide an amputee with a prosthetic device that would come as close as possible to replicating the movement and functional value of a real limb, scientists and doctors began to work together at understanding the range of motion peculiar to the human body.

Sports can be categorized according to the kinds of movements used. Each individual sport uses a unique combination of basic motions, including walking, running, jumping, kicking, and throwing. These basic motions have all been rigidly defined for scientific study so that injuries related to these motions can be better understood and treated. For example, sports that place heavy demands on one part of an athlete's body may overload that part and produce an injury, such as "tennis elbow" and "swimmer's shoulder." Baseball, on the other hand, is a throwing sport and certain injuries from overuse of the shoulder and elbow are expected. Athletes who play volleyball or golf also use some variation of the throwing motion and therefore sustain injuries to their shoulders and elbows.

Today, sports medicine concentrates on the treatment and prevention of injuries sustained while participating in sports. Sports medicine is not a single career but a group of careers that is concerned with the health of the athlete. For its specific purposes, the field of sports medicine defines *athlete* as both the amateur athlete who exercises for health and recreation, and the elite athlete who is involved in sports at the collegiate, Olympic, or professional level. Sports physicians treat people of all ages and abilities, including those with disabilities.

Among the professions in the field of sports medicine are the trainer, physical therapist, physiologist, biomechanical engineer, nutritionist, psychologist, and physician. In addition, the field of sports medicine also encompasses the work of those who conduct research to determine the causes of sports injuries. Discoveries made by researchers in sports medicine have spread from orthopedics to almost every branch of medicine.

Arthroscopic surgery falls into this category. It was developed by orthopedic surgeons to see and operate on skeletal joints without a large open incision. The arthroscope itself is a slender cylinder with a series of lenses that transmit the image from the joint to the eye. The lens system is surrounded by glass fibers designed to transfer light from an external source to the joint. Inserted into the joint through one small, dime- to quarter-sized incision, the arthroscope functions as the surgeon's "eyes" to allow pinpoint accuracy when operating. The surgical elements, themselves, are inserted through other small incisions nearby. In the 1970s only a few surgeons used the techniques of arthroscopy and did so as an exploratory measure to determine whether or not traditional surgery had a good chance of succeeding. Today, arthroscopy is the most commonly performed orthopedic surgery performed in the United States; instead of being an exploratory procedure, 80 percent of all arthroscopic surgeries are performed to repair tissue damage.

THE JOB

Sports physicians treat the injuries and illnesses of both the amateur and elite athlete. They are often referred to as team physicians. Depending upon the level of athlete they are treating, sports physicians are usually either practitioners in family practice as medical doctors (*M.D.'s*) or *orthopedic surgeons*. More often than not, the individual who works as the team physician for a professional sports team is too busy tending to the health needs of the team to have time for a private practice as well.

Brent Rich, M.D., team physician for Brigham Young University, agrees that there are some varieties of sports physicians: "Sports physicians come in two major varieties: primary care providers with training in nonsurgical sports medicine and orthopedic surgeons. The majority of sports physicians are in private practice. Each area has its rewards and downfalls. As a board-certified family physician, I deal with about 90 percent of what goes on in the sports medicine arena."

At the scholastic level, the team physician is usually the *school physician* and is appointed by the school board. Athletic programs at the collegiate level are usually capable of supporting a staff of one or more physicians who cater to the needs of the athletic teams. The size of the school and athletic program also determines the number of full-time physicians; for example, a state university basketball team might have one physician, even an orthopedic surgeon, dedicated wholly to that team's needs.

Professional teams, of course, have the necessary resources to employ both a full-time physician and an orthopedic surgeon. Generally, their presence is required at all practices and games. Often, professional teams have a sports medicine department to handle the various aspects of treatment, from training to nutrition to mental health. If they don't have their own department, they take advantage of the specialists at university hospitals and private care facilities in the area.

To fully understand the nature of a particular sports injury, sports physicians study the athlete as well as the sport. The musculoskeletal system is a complex organization of muscle segments, each related to the function of others through connecting bones and articulations. Pathological states of the musculoskeletal system are reflected in deficits (weaknesses in key muscle segments) that may actually be quite distant from the site of the injury or trauma. The risk factors for any given sport can be assessed by comparing the performance demands that regularly produce characteristic injuries with the risk factors that might predispose an athlete to injury.

Strength and flexibility, for example, are requirements for nearly every sport. Stronger muscles improve an athlete's performance, and deficits in strength can leave him or her prone to injury. Rehabilitation under the supervision of a sports physician focuses on rebuilding lost muscle strength. Likewise, an athlete who lacks flexibility may subject him or herself to strains or pulls on his or her muscles. For this athlete, rehabilitation would center on warming and stretching the isolated muscles, as well as muscle groups, to reduce or alleviate such muscle strains. In both cases, it is the responsibility of the sports physician to analyze the potential for injury and work with other sports health professionals to prevent it, as well as to treat the injury after it happens. The goal of every sports physician is to keep athletes performing to the best of their ability and to rehabilitate them safely and quickly after they are injured.

To prevent injuries, as well as treat them, sports physicians administer or supervise physical examinations of the athletes under their care to determine the fitness level of each athlete prior to that athlete actively pursuing the sport. During the exams, sports physicians note any physical traits, defects, previous injuries, or weaknesses. They also check the player's maturity, coordination, stamina, balance, strength, and emotional state. The physical examination accomplishes many different goals. To begin with, it quickly establishes the athlete's state of health and allows the sports physician to determine whether that athlete is physically capable of playing his or her sport. On the basis of the physical exam, the sports physician advises the coach on the fitness level of the athlete, which in turn determines a great deal about the athlete's position on the team. Furthermore, the exam alerts the sports physician to signs of injury, both old and new. Old or existing injuries can be noted and put under observation, and weaknesses can be detected early on so that coach and trainers can implement proper conditioning and training patterns.

Depending upon the results of their physical examinations, the sports physician may advise athletes to gain or lose weight, change their eating, drinking, and sleeping habits, or alter their training programs to include more strength or cardiovascular exercises. Routine physical checkups are also a common way of evaluating an athlete's performance level throughout a season, and many sports physicians will administer several exams to gauge the effect of their advice, as well as to ensure that the athlete is making the suggested changes in habits or training.

Preventing injuries is the sports physician's first goal and conditioning is probably the best way to accomplish that goal. Sports physicians are often responsible for developing and supervising the conditioning and training programs that other sports health professionals will implement. The sports physician may work with the coaching staff and athletic trainers to help athletes develop strength, cardiovascular fitness, and flexibility, or the sports physician may advise the coaching and training staff members of the overall safety of a practice program. For example, the sports physician may evaluate the drills and practice exercises that a football coach is using on a given day to make certain that the exercises won't exacerbate old injuries or cause new ones. Sports physicians may even be involved in the selection of protective gear and equipment. The degree of their involvement, again, depends on the size of the team and the nature of the physicians' skills or expertise, as well as on the number of other people on the staff. Large, professional teams tend to have equally large staffs on which one person alone is responsible for ordering and maintaining the protective gear.

Sports physicians are often in attendance at practices (or they are nearby, in case of an injury), but their presence at games is mandatory. If a player shows signs of undue fatigue, exhaustion, or injury, the sports physician needs to be there to remove the athlete from the competition. Dr. Rich says being at the games is one of the perks of his profession: "To see others accomplish what they desire gives me satisfaction. Another good part is covering sports events and feeling a part of the action on the sidelines, in the locker room, or in the heat of the battle."

After an athlete is injured, the sports physician must be capable of immediately administering first aid or other procedures. He or she first examines the athlete to determine the gravity and extent of the injury. If the damage is extreme enough (or cannot be determined from a manual and visual exam), the sports physician may send the athlete to the hospital for X rays or other diagnostic examinations. Later, the team physician may perform surgery or recommend that the athlete undergo treatment or surgery by a specialist. Some of the most common types of injuries are stress fractures, knee injuries, back injuries, shoulder injuries, and elbow injuries.

The sports physician oversees the athlete's recuperation and rehabilitation following an injury, including the nature and timing of physical therapy. The athlete's return to practice and competition is determined by the sports physician's analysis of the athlete's progress. Frequent physical examinations allow the physician to judge whether or not the athlete is fit enough to return to full activity. The decision to allow an athlete to compete again following an injury is a responsibility that sports physicians take seriously; whether the athlete is an amateur or an elite professional, the future health and well-being of the athlete is at stake and cannot be risked, even for an important championship game.

A developing area of the sports physician's responsibilities is the diagnosis and treatment of substance-abuse problems. Unfortunately, even as research on the field of sports medicine has produced new methods and medications that mask pain and decrease inflammation—which shortens recovery time and lengthens athletic careers—some also produce unnatural performance enhancement. Most notable of these are anabolic steroids—synthetic modifications of the male hormone, testosterone—which have become widely abused by athletes who use them to better their performances. When taken while on a high-protein diet and an intensive exercise regimen, these drugs can increase muscle bulk, which in turn can produce increased strength, speed, and stamina. The side effects of these drugs, however, include aggression, sterility, liver problems, premature closure of the growth plates of the long bones, and in women, male pattern baldness and facial hair. These side effects are usually irreversible and, as such, pose a significant health risk for young athletes.

Another method also banned from use in competition-level athletics is the withdrawal of an athlete's blood several weeks prior to competition. The blood is stored and then, just before the athlete competes, the blood is transfused back into his or her bloodstream. This process, blood doping, also has serious, even fatal, side effects, including heart failure and death.

Finally, professional athletes sometimes develop substance-abuse problems, such as alcohol or drug abuse. Sports physicians are responsible for detecting all of these problems and helping the athlete return to a healthy lifestyle, which may or may not include competing in their sport.

In addition to the responsibilities and duties outlined above, many sports physicians also perform clinical studies and work with researchers to determine ways of improving sports medicine practices. Often, the results of such studies and research are published in medical journals and popular magazines.

REQUIREMENTS
High School
During high school, take as many health and sports-related classes as possible. Biology, chemistry, health, computers, and English are important core courses. High grades in high school are important for anyone aspiring to join the medical profession, because competition for acceptance into medical programs at colleges and universities is always tough.

Postsecondary Training
Sports physicians have either an M.D. (medical doctor degree) or a D.O. (doctor of osteopathy degree). Each involves completing four years of college, followed by four years of medical school, study and internship at an accredited medical school, and up to six years of residency training in a medical specialty, such as surgery. Many physicians also complete a fellowship in sports medicine either during or after their residency.

During the first two years of medical school, medical students usually spend most of their time in classrooms learning anatomy, physiology, biology, and chemistry, among other subjects. In their last two years, they begin seeing patients in a clinic, observing and working with doctors to treat patients and develop their diagnostic skills. Some medical schools are beginning to alter this time-honored tradition by having medical students begin to work with patients much sooner than two years into their schooling, but this method of combining classroom and clinical experiences is not yet fully accepted or integrated into the curriculum.

After medical school, the new doctors spend a year in an internship program, followed by several years in a residency training program in their area of specialty. Most sports physicians complete this stage of their training by working in orthopedics or general practice.

The fellowship portion of a doctor's training is essential if he or she has chosen to specialize. For example, the doctor specializing in general surgery and interested in sports medicine would probably seek an orthopedics fellowship providing further training in orthopedic surgery techniques.

Certification or Licensing
Sports physicians can become board certified in orthopaedic sports medicine by the American Board of Orthopaedic Surgery. Contact the board for more information on certification requirements.

To become licensed, doctors must have completed the above training (detailed in Postsecondary Training) in accordance with the guidelines and rules of their chosen area or specialty. Beyond the formal requirements, this usually involves a qualifying written exam, followed by in-depth oral examinations designed to test the candidate's knowledge and expertise.

Other Requirements

To be a successful sports physician, you must be able to learn and remember all the many parts of the human body and how they function together. Knowledge of different sports and their demands on an athlete's body is also important. Like all medical doctors, you need to be able to communicate clearly to your patients with compassion and understanding.

EXPLORING

High school students interested in becoming sports physicians should look into the possibility of working with the physician, coach, or athletic trainer for one of their school's teams. Firsthand experience is the best way to gain fresh perspective into the role of the team physician. Later on, when applying for other paid or volunteer positions, it will help to have already had sports-related experience. Dr. Rich agrees, "Try to get experience with a physician who does what you think you want to do. Spending time in their offices, in surgery, or on the sidelines at high school games will give you exposure. As you learn more, you can do more."

EMPLOYERS

Most sports physicians are in private practice, so they work for themselves or with other medical doctors. Some sports physicians, however, may work for sports clinics, rehabilitation centers, hospitals, and college/university teaching hospitals. Still other sports physicians travel with professional baseball, basketball, football, hockey, and soccer teams to attend to those specific athletes. Sports physicians are employed all over the country.

STARTING OUT

You won't become the team physician for a National Basketball Association team fresh out of medical school. Many sports physicians begin by joining an existing practice and volunteering with a local sports organization. After several years, they may apply to the school board for consideration as a team physician for their local school district. Later, they may apply for a position with a college team until they ultimately seek a position with a national or international professional athletics team or organization. This gradual climb occurs while the individual also pursues a successful private practice and builds a strong, solid reputation. Often, the sports physician's established reputation in an area of specialty draws the attention of coaches and management looking to hire a physician for their team. Others take a more aggressive and ambitious route and immediately begin applying for positions with various professional sports teams as an assistant team physician. As in any other field, contacts can prove to be extremely useful, as are previous experiences in the field. For example, a summer internship during high school or college with a professional hockey team might lead to a job possibility with that hockey team years later. Employment opportunities depend on the skill and ambitions of each job candidate.

ADVANCEMENT

Depending on the nature of an aspiring sports physician's affiliation with athletic organizations (part time or full time), advancement paths will vary. For most sports physicians, advancement will accompany the successful development of their private practices. For those few sports physicians who are employed full time by professional athletic organizations, advancement from assistant to team physician is usually accompanied by increased responsibilities and a corresponding increase in salary.

EARNINGS

The earnings of a sports physician vary depending upon his or her responsibilities and the size and nature of the team. The private sports physician of a professional individual athlete, such as a figure skater or long-distance runner, will most likely earn far less than the team physician for a professional football or basketball team, primarily because the earnings of the team are so much greater so the organization can afford to pay more for the physician's services. On the other hand, the team physician for the professional basketball team probably wouldn't have time for a private practice, although the sports physician for the figure skater or runner would, in all likelihood, also have a private practice or work for a sports health facility.

According to the U.S. Department of Labor, general practitioners and family practice physicians earned a mean income of approximately $149,850 in 2006. Ten percent of these physicians earned less than $69,990 annually in that same year, and some earned significantly more. This general figure does not include the fees and other income sports physicians receive from the various athletic organizations for whom they work. Again, these fees will vary according to the size of the team, the location, and the level of the athletic organization (high school, college, or professional, being the most common). The income generated from these fees is far less than what they earn in their private practices. On the other hand, those team physicians who are employed full time by a professional organization will likely make more than their nonprofessional sports counterparts, even as much as $1 million or more.

WORK ENVIRONMENT

Sports physicians must be ready for a variety of work conditions, from the sterile, well-lighted hospital operating room to the concrete bleachers at an outdoor municipal swimming pool. The work environment is as diverse as the sports in which athletes are involved. Although most of their day-to-day responsibilities will be carried out in clean, comfortable surroundings, on game day sports physicians are expected to be where the athletes are, and that might be a muddy field (football and soccer); a snow-covered forest (cross-country skiing); a hot, dusty track (track and field); or a steamy ring (boxing). Picture the playing field of any given sport and that is where you will find sports physicians. They are also expected to travel with the athletes whenever they go out of town. This means being away from their home and family, often for several days, depending on the nature, level, and location of the competition.

OUTLOOK

After years of watching athletes close down the bars after a game, coaches and management now realize the benefits of good health and nutrition. Within the world of professional sports, the word is out: Proper nutrition, conditioning, and training prevent injuries to athletes, and preventing injuries is the key when those athletes are making their owners revenues in the billions of dollars. A top sports physician, then, is a worthwhile investment for any professional team. Thus, the outlook for sports physicians remains strong.

Even outside the realm of professional sports, amateur athletes require the skills and expertise of talented sports physicians to handle the aches and pains that come from pulling muscles and overtaxing aging knees. Athletes of all ages and abilities take their competitions seriously, and are as prone to injury as any professional athlete, if not more, because amateur athletes in general spend less time conditioning their bodies.

FOR MORE INFORMATION

To obtain publications about sports medicine, contact
American College of Sports Medicine
PO Box 1440
Indianapolis, IN 46206-1440
Tel: 317-637-9200
http://www.acsm.org

To join a forum on various medical issues, visit the AMA's Web site.
American Medical Association (AMA)
515 North State Street
Chicago, IL 60610-5453
Tel: 800-621-8335
http://www.ama-assn.org

For general information on sports medicine, contact
American Orthopaedic Society for Sports Medicine
6300 North River Road, Suite 500
Rosemont, IL 60018-4206
Tel: 847-292-4900
Email: aossm@aossm.org
http://www.sportsmed.org

For a list of accredited athletic training programs, job listings, and information on certification for athletic trainers, contact
National Athletic Trainers' Association
2952 Stemmons Freeway
Dallas, TX 75247-6916
Tel: 214-637-6282
http://www.nata.org

Sports Publicists

QUICK FACTS

School Subjects
English
Journalism
Speech

Personal Skills
Communication/ideas
Leadership/management

Work Environment
Primarily indoors
One location with some
  travel

Minimum Education Level
Bachelor's degree

Salary Range
$20,000 to $60,000 to
$250,000+

Certification or Licensing
Voluntary

Outlook
About as fast as the average

DOT
N/A

GOE
13.01.01

NOC
5124

O*NET-SOC
11-2031.00

OVERVIEW

There are two types of *sports publicists*: those who work for professional and amateur teams and those who work for individual professional athletes. *Sports team publicists* handle the daily press operations for the organization. They handle the media relations, set up interviews with players, ensure that the correct information is distributed to the press, and write press releases. *Individual sports publicists*, who work for individual players, try to enhance their client's image by casting them in a positive light via newspaper, magazine, and television stories. Sports publicists are sometimes called *sports information directors, press agents, public relations (PR) directors, marketing directors,* or *directors of communication.*

HISTORY

Sports have matured into one of our nation's largest businesses. Professional teams are the most widely recognized industry segment in sports. Professional teams include all of the various sports teams, leagues, and governing bodies for which individuals get paid for their performance. Some of the most notable organizations include the National Football League, National Basketball Association, National Hockey League, and Major League Baseball. These are commonly known as the four majors. During recent decades, more professional leagues have started, such as the Women's National Basketball Association, the Arena Football League, and Major League Soccer. There are also many minor league and collegiate organizations.

THE JOB

Sports publicists are responsible for all of the team's publications, including media guides, programs for all home games, schedule cards, mail order brochures, recruiting kits, annual reports, and booster club newsletters. They also handle all of the team's publicity, which includes news and feature releases, news conferences and background information, photography, media interviews, and media tours.

Sports publicists also deal with game management, which includes announcers, scoreboard operations, telephone hook-ups, scorers, officiating facilities, press box seating and credentials, broadcast facilities, video facilities, and travel and lodging. They also are in charge of generating crowd participation by developing promotions, giveaways, half-time exhibitions, and music. Publicists also help design the team's uniform insignia and team banners.

Sports information directors might have other responsibilities, such as creating and placing advertising, attending league meetings, conventions, and workshops, coordinating booster club activities, fund-raising, fan surveys, budgets, equipment negotiations, licensing, and merchandising. Unlike other public relations practitioners, most sports information directors promote their competition as well as the team they work for. The better the opposition, the better the fan interest and ticket sales.

Collegiate publicists might not be affiliated with the college or university's public relations department, but instead might be housed under the athletic department.

Publicists who work for athletes constantly create publicity and news events to get their clients into the spotlight. Many publicists try to show their clients in a positive light by having the athletes participate in goodwill appearances or work with organizations like the United Way. Maintaining a positive image increases the athletes' potential income and market value.

REQUIREMENTS

High School

As a sports publicist, you are the voice of the person or team that you represent, so being an effective communicator is very important. Take classes in English and journalism to hone your writing skills, and take speech classes to help you learn how to compose your ideas and thoughts and convey them to an audience. You should also take other college preparatory classes, such as math, science, and foreign language. Since you will be dealing with the public, a general knowledge of history, sociology, psychology, and current events will be especially important.

Postsecondary Training

Most publicists working in the sports industry are college graduates with degrees in public relations, marketing, communications, journalism, or sports administration. A college degree is essential, according to the Public Relations Society of America.

Certification or Licensing

The Public Relations Society of America offers voluntary certification to public relations specialists. While this certification is not sports-related, it will help show prospective employers that you possess a high level of knowledge and experience. Candidates who pass a written and oral examination are designated as accredited in public relations.

Other Requirements

In order to be a successful sports publicist, you should be outgoing and able to get along with many different types of people. Participate in sports or be a team manager in high school or college so that you become familiar with the lifestyle of an athlete and you can relate to it. You should also be organized and able to work well under stress, since you will likely be dealing with big-name clients.

EXPLORING

Ask your teacher or counselor to set up an information interview with a publicist. Volunteer to handle various public relations-type duties for your high school sports teams or clubs. Run for student council or another leadership position at school to gain experience with public speaking and management. Read publications such as *Sports Illustrated* (http://www.si.com) and *Sports Business Journal* (http://www.sportsbusinessjournal.com), and attend sporting events so that you stay current on sports knowledge. It is also a good idea to volunteer to assist your school's athletic department (in high school or college); you may be able to have a hand in developing a team's media guide or programs. Cover sports for your college newspaper so that you will have some clips to show employers.

EMPLOYERS

Sports publicists work in one of three areas. Some work for public relations firms that handle athletes or sports-oriented events. Others work directly for sports teams in their front offices. Some are self-employed, working directly with clients.

Books to Read: Sports Fiction

Coy, John. *Crackback*. New York: Scholastic Paperbacks, 2007.
Crutcher, Chris. *Athletic Shorts: Six Short Stories*. New York: HarperTeen, 2002.
Crutcher, Chris. *Running Loose*. New York: HarperTeen, 2003.
Harris, Mark. *Bang the Drum Slowly*. Lincoln, Nebr.: Bison Books, 2003.
Kinsella, W. P. *Shoeless Joe*. Boston: Houghton Mifflin, 1999.
Levy, Marilyn. *Run for Your Life*. New York: Penguin, 1997.
Lipsyte, Robert. *Yellow Flag*. New York: HarperTeen, 2007.
Malamud, Bernard. *The Natural*. New York: Farrar, Straus & Giroux, 2003.
Martino, Alfred C. *Pinned*. New York: Harcourt Paperbacks, 2006.

STARTING OUT

The best way to enter public relations at the professional sports level is by gaining experience at the collegiate ranks. Many internships are available at this level, and getting one is the best way to get your foot in the door. As an intern, you may be asked to contribute to publications and to write and prepare press releases. This experience will give you a great opportunity not only to learn how to generate all of this material, but also to begin collecting samples of your writing and to develop your clip file. Every interviewer you will meet will ask you for your clip file, since they provide proof of your journalistic and PR writing skills.

There are also training programs within established public relations companies.

ADVANCEMENT

"Like baseball players, front office staff generally look to advance to higher levels, from single-A to double-A or triple-A onto the majors," says Gary Radke, former marketing director of the Wisconsin Timber Rattlers minor league baseball team. "Within the given organizations, there really isn't much in the way of advancement because everyone is basically at the same level. Upper-management positions are the general manager and assistant general manager."

EARNINGS

Sports publicists can earn anywhere from $20,000 to more than $250,000 per year. People just starting out might make less, while those with proven track records command higher salaries. Publicists who work for individual athletes can earn more money.

"Minor league marketing directors make anywhere from $21,000 up to $60,000," says Gary Radke. "I received health insurance, 10 sick days, two personal days, apparel discounts, health club memberships, and free soda at the games."

WORK ENVIRONMENT

During the season, sports publicists may work 12- to 20-hour days, seven days a week. Since most sporting events take place in the evening or on weekends, and half are played on the road, sports publicists spend a lot of time on the job. Some publicists travel with their teams, while others do not. Either way, this job is very time consuming.

OUTLOOK

The field of sports publicity is very competitive, and even though it is expanding as more teams and leagues form, it is still difficult to land a job. The U.S. Department of Labor predicts that employment of public relations specialists in general is expected to increase faster than the average for all occupations through 2014, but the number of applicants with degrees in the communications fields (journalism, public relations, and advertising) is expected to exceed the number of job openings.

FOR MORE INFORMATION

For information on careers at the collegiate level, contact
College Sports Information Directors of America
http://www.cosida.com

For information on careers and certification in public relations, contact
The Public Relations Society of America
33 Maiden Lane, 11th Floor
New York, NY 10038-4518
Tel: 212-460-1400
http://www.prsa.org

Sports Scouts

OVERVIEW

Sports scouts observe athletic contests to gather information that will help the team that employs them. They may attend a game in the hopes of recruiting a player, or they may accumulate information about an opponent's players and strategies. There are approximately 1,000 professional sports scouts in the United States.

HISTORY

In the first part of the 20th century, baseball became popular as a professional sport. Large eastern cities like New York and Boston were home to some of the best and most popular teams. While these teams competed in baseball stadiums, their scouts were competing to find talented, young players.

Traveling by train through the South and Midwest, baseball scouts rushed from town to town in hopes of discovering the next Cy Young or Cap Anson.

Some scouts worked for professional teams while others signed players to personal contracts, hoping to sell those contracts to the owners of professional teams. As baseball became more organized, scouts began to work almost exclusively for one professional team. Soon, young prospects no longer were sent directly to Major League Baseball teams, but played in the minor leagues or farm teams. These teams were set up to teach players, who already possessed excellent abilities, the subtle nuances of the game.

These new teams created a need for even more scouts. In addition to locating and signing talented young players, other scouts were assigned the task of watching these players develop and deciding when they were ready to advance to the next level.

QUICK FACTS

School Subjects
Foreign language
Mathematics
Psychology

Personal Skills
Leadership/management

Work Environment
Indoors and outdoors
Primarily multiple locations

Minimum Education Level
High school diploma

Salary Range
$13,990 to $26,950 to $58,890+

Certification or Licensing
None available

Outlook
More slowly than the average

DOT
153

GOE
01.10.01

NOC
5252

O*NET-SOC
27-2022.00

As football, basketball, and soccer became popular sports, professional teams began to hire scouts to evaluate the talent of players and the strengths and weaknesses of other teams.

THE JOB

Sports scouts attend sporting events and record their findings for pay. They may travel from city to city watching other teams from their league play, or they may attend games for the purpose of recruiting players for their own team. Scouts are an extension of the coaching staff of a team, and in many cases, assistant coaches have scouting responsibilities.

There are two general tasks assigned to scouts. One is recruitment; the other is to gather information about an opposing team. *Recruitment scouts* attend high school and college games to look for talented young players. Coaches or general managers from professional teams may inform scouts about specific personnel needs. For example, a basketball coach may need a guard who can handle the ball well and shoot jump shots. A scout attends numerous college games and then returns to the coach with a list of players who meet the description. In most cases, the list returned will rate the individual players and include some additional information, such as the players' ages, heights, and weights. Notes or impressions from an interview the scout conducted with the player would also be included. Recruitment scouts may attend a game to see a particular individual play but will also make notes on other players. Scouts may see 10 or more games a week, so they must keep detailed notes. Scouts must also be comfortable with statistics, both compiling and understanding them. Scouts examine statistics like earned run average, yards per carry, and field goal percentage in order to assist them in their deliberations concerning players.

A scout may need to see a player more than once to determine if he or she has the ability to play at the next level. Scouts report their findings back to the coach or general manager, and it is up to that person to act on the scout's recommendations.

Recruitment scouts need to see numerous games so that they acquire the ability to accurately assess talent. Scouts need to distinguish between players who have sound, fundamental skills and an understanding of the game and players who are natural athletes but have not yet acquired the finer skills.

Many professional sports leagues have minor leagues or developmental leagues in which players not yet good enough to play at the highest professional level hone their skills. Professional baseball has minor leagues, or a farm system, that consists of players who have talent but are still maturing or learning skills. Many scouts are assigned to these leagues to keep a watchful eye on players as they develop. For example, a Major League Baseball team may employ both full- and part-time scouts, most of whom concentrate on players already playing in the minor leagues. They also receive a daily report compiled by the Major League Scouting Bureau (MLSB). The MLSB is a professional scouting organization overseen by the Commissioner's Office of Major League Baseball. It employs approximately 34 full-time scouts and 13 part-time scouts. Other professional sports leagues have similar systems.

Assistant coaches and *scouts* often attend opponents' games to find out about players' abilities and team strategies. They watch the game, diagram set plays, and note players' tendencies. During practice the following week, scouts share their findings and, when possible, detail plans to help offset an opponent's strength.

REQUIREMENTS

There are no educational requirements for becoming a sports scout. Most scouts are former players or coaches in the particular sport in which they work.

High School

A general high school education will give you the basic skills you need to succeed in sports scouting. Speech and English courses will help you communicate easily with prospects as well as relay your findings to coaches, managers, and front office workers. Learn Spanish or Japanese to help you connect with foreign players, who are increasingly sought after by professional sports teams. Finally, take physical education classes and join sports teams—especially the sport for which you want to scout.

Postsecondary Training

There are no colleges and universities that offer classes in sports scouting. Professional baseball teams do send promising employees to a "scout school" that is sponsored by the Major League Scouting Bureau. Employees learn the basics of scouting and how to judge talent. The most famous graduate of the school is former scout and current White Sox General Manager Kenny Williams.

Other Requirements

First and foremost, a person who would like to become a sports scout should have vast knowledge of a particular sport. For a sports scout, an athletic contest is not only something to enjoy, but something to study. To be a successful sports scout, you need to be detail oriented and methodical in order to understand the rules, regulations, fundamentals, strategies, and personality types that are best suited to athletic competition.

You also need to have above-average organizational skills. More often than not, you will attend several games before reporting to a supervisor. You must be able to organize your thoughts and notes so that you can compare players from several games to come to conclusions about their abilities.

Communication skills are very important. You should be able to write and speak well. You will interact with other coaches and players on a daily basis. If you work as a recruitment scout, you will be in contact with younger players, and so it would be helpful to be able to work well with and understand younger people. A proficiency in a foreign language, especially Spanish or Japanese, will be also of great help, since you will be sent to foreign countries to monitor the development of promising athletes.

You should also be a team player, a good judge of talent and character, and be able to recognize ability and mental toughness in others.

EXPLORING

It goes without saying that individuals interested in a career as a sports scout should participate in sporting events at the high school and college level. You can participate either as a player or as an assistant to players or coaches. You should read a variety of books by coaches and athletes to learn fundamentals and strategies. Also, take part in community sports programs to interact with a variety of players and observe different styles of play.

EMPLOYERS

Sports scouts are employed by major league organizations throughout North America and the world. Others work for professional scouting organizations, such as the Major League Scouting Bureau.

STARTING OUT

Many sports scouts are former athletes who have retired from playing and use their knowledge of the game to scout for younger talent. Not only do athletes gain knowledge from years of competition, but they make valuable contacts in the sporting world.

An aspiring sports scout should become familiar with local sports activity and keep track of talented young players. Meeting people who are active in the sports community is a great help. Sports scouts are part of a vast network of people who gather, compile, and exchange information about sports. Coaches, broadcasters, and journalists are also members of this group.

ADVANCEMENT

Sports scouts who provide accurate and concise reports often have the opportunity to observe more talented athletes. A professional baseball scout, for example, may begin scouting college players. As the scout gains experience in providing reliable information, they may be assigned to a minor league division, and eventually may become the director of scouting for a major league team.

Scouts who succeed and advance are organized, honest, and effective communicators. Sports scouts build their reputations by identifying players who will be successful at the professional level. Advancement is often based on the success of the players whom the scout has selected.

EARNINGS

According to the U.S. Department of Labor, sports scouts and coaches had median annual earnings of $26,950 in 2006. Beginning sports scouts and coaches earned salaries of $13,990 or less, while the most experienced scouts with many success stories earned more than $58,890. Sports scouts also are reimbursed for travel expenses and meals. Another fringe benefit is free admission to countless sporting events.

Many sports scouts also receive such fringe benefits as paid vacation and sick days, health insurance, and pension plans.

WORK ENVIRONMENT

Sports scouts travel an average of three weeks out of every month, and they are away from home most nights and weekends. While on the road, they stay in hotels and eat most of their meals in restaurants. They travel often by car or bus and also frequently by plane.

Workdays on the road are quite long. A sports scout may be on the road by 7:00 A.M. to drive four hours to meet with a player and watch an afternoon game. There may be another game to see that night in another location, or the evening may be spent reviewing tape of games attended over the last few days.

Long hours and near constant travel are typical of work as a sports scout, and more often than not, there is little reward for the effort. A scout may recommend several hundred players over the course of their career and only a handful of those players will ever make it to the professional level. Despite this, dedicated sports scouts continue to visit isolated diamonds, tiny high school and college gyms, and the cracked concrete of the urban ball court looking for the next superstar.

OUTLOOK

There will be little change in the number of sports scouts employed in North America. There are approximately 1,000 professional sports scouts in the United States and most work for professional teams. Baseball is the sport that employs the greatest number of scouts.

A relatively new concept in the industry is pool scouting. The concept involves a group of scouts who collect data on a great many players and provide that information to several teams. The scouts are not employed by any one team, but by professional scouting organizations, such as the Major League Scouting Bureau.

As professional leagues add expansion teams and the talent pool diminishes, there will probably be more opportunities for sports scouts to travel and work in foreign countries. On the other hand, if professional sports leagues contract, there will be fewer job opportunities for scouts.

FOR MORE INFORMATION

For information on baseball scouting, contact
Major League Scouting Bureau
3500 Porsche Way, Suite 100
Ontario, CA 91764-4941
Tel: 909-980-1881
http://mlb.mlb.com/mlb/official_info/about_mlb/index.jsp

Contact the following organizations for information on scouting careers:
National Basketball Association
645 Fifth Avenue
New York, NY 10022-5910
Tel: 212-826-7000
http://www.nba.com

National Football League
410 Park Avenue
New York, NY 10022-4407
Tel: 212-758-1500
http://www.nfl.com

Sports Statisticians

OVERVIEW

Sports statisticians compute and record the statistics relating to a particular sports event, game, or competition, or the accomplishments of a team or single athlete during competition. They do this manually or by using calculators or computers. There are approximately 19,000 statisticians in the United States, but sports statisticians make up only a very small portion of this group.

HISTORY

Statistics is a relatively new science relating to the collection and interpretation of data. Ancient record-keeping can be traced back to the Old Testament and to population records compiled by the Babylonians and the Romans. Formal population studies in a scientific sense, however, were only begun early in the 19th century in the United States and certain European countries. The motivation for such statistics was primarily to promote efficient bureaucracies, but statistical studies were conducted to try to solve other problems, in fields as diverse as social science, biology, and physics.

In the late 19th century, British statistician Sir Ronald Aylmer Fisher began his investigations on experimental designs, randomization, and mathematical statistics. Fisher and others developed small-sample statistical techniques and methods, such as the analysis of variance and covariance. His contributions are regarded by many as the origin of modern statistics. Since then, the field of statistics has grown rapidly, and statistics are used in nearly every area of study, from agriculture to health science to sports.

Sports fans, athletes, and coaches have kept informal records of the best and worst performances since before organized sports began.

QUICK FACTS

School Subjects
Computer science
Mathematics

Personal Skills
Leadership/management

Work Environment
Indoors and outdoors
Primarily multiple locations

Minimum Education Level
High school diploma

Salary Range
$5,000 to $35,000 to $108,630+

Certification or Licensing
None available

Outlook
About as fast as the average

DOT
020

GOE
02.06.02

NOC
2161

O*NET-SOC
15-2041.00

Early in the 19th century, as the rules and regulations of different sports began to be organized by official gaming associations, the importance of official record-keeping was recognized. Soon, statistics were not only a vital resource when deciding which records were set or broken, but they were being used to help determine the outcome of specific plays. For example, during a basketball game the referee asks the official scorer and statistician how many time-outs the home team has already taken or how many fouls a certain player has received.

Once, the statistician sat in the bleachers or on the bench, marking up a scoring book with slashes and checks to indicate runs, goals, fouls, etc. Later, the statistician would tally up the various totals, computing team averages as well as individual play averages. Today, professional sports associations and leagues have highly sophisticated computers and programs that instantly tally the totals, averages, and percentages at the touch of a button.

THE JOB

Sports statisticians compute and record the statistics relating to a particular sports event, game, or competition, or the accomplishments of a team or single athlete during competition. They use their own knowledge of basic math and algebraic formulas, alone or in combination with calculators and computers, to calculate the statistics related to a particular sport or athlete.

Most high school, college, and professional team sports have an *official scorer or official statistician* who attends every home game and sits courtside, at what is called the scorer's table. The *team statistician* running stats at a basketball game, for example, keeps track of the score, the number of time-outs, and specific calls made by the referees, such as team and player fouls. The statistician is also referred to as the official scorer because if any item on the scoreboard is questioned by a referee, one of the coaches, or another game official, the individual who ultimately has the power to determine the outcome is the statistician.

Many statisticians still work by hand with a special notebook for recording the game statistics. As each play and call occurs in the game, the statistician records the play or call in a particular column or row of the stat book. Later, the statistician will make a tally of the total number of player errors, rebounds, assists, goals, etc. He or she can determine such statistics as the average number of rebounds in a quarter or per game. The statistician uses the same, predetermined algebraic formulas to compute the statistics for a single athlete or an entire team. Usually, the statistician keeps the stats, for both the home team and the visiting team, by individual. At the end of the game, the statistician can then provide both coaches and teams with specific information on their respective play during the game.

Other statisticians use computers with specialized software programs that automatically compute the player and team statistics. Most professional athletic teams have both a manual scorer and one or more individuals keeping statistics with the league- or association-sponsored statistics program. For example, both the National Basketball Association (NBA) and the National Football League (NFL) have computerized statistics programs that are used throughout the league or association. These programs, created by independent, private companies, allow each team to choose the statisticians who will run the system, while ensuring that the statistics systems used will be universal. One such company, SuperStats, created the computerized system for the NFL. In many cases, the computer system that calculates the different statistics also controls the different scoreboards in the arena or stadium and can quickly and efficiently produce flash and quarter stats for the teams, coaching staff, and various members of the media.

In professional team sports, the home team is responsible for making certain an official scorer/statistician is in attendance at all home games. The away or visiting team may have its own statistician or staff of statisticians, but the individual responsible for the official scores, etc., is hired by the home team, and this is usually the same person throughout an entire season.

Statisticians begin work by arriving at the arena or stadium in plenty of time to set up, greet the officials, peruse any announcements or press releases from the public relations offices of the home or visiting team, and get the starting lineups from both the home and visiting team coaches. Statisticians who work with computer equipment may arrive even earlier to set up their equipment and make sure the system is up and running well in advance of game time.

Once the game begins, statisticians quite literally cannot take their eyes off the game. They need to see every play as it happens in order to record it precisely in the stat book or computer. Often, the official team scorer or statistician keeps track of certain statistics, while other statisticians keep track of the remaining statistics. For example, the official team scorer for a professional basketball team is responsible for tracking the field goals attempted and the field goals made, the three-point shots attempted and made, the free throws attempted and made, the number of personal fouls, and the number of time-outs taken. He or she may record other statistics, but if there is a discrepancy it is these stats for which he or she is responsible during the game. A team of statisticians who work the computers are responsible for taking down the number of rebounds, assists, steals, and so on. The most important aspect of the job is to remember that the statistician is doing more than compiling statistics; the statistician is recording the game, event by event.

Statisticians also work for television and radio stations and the sports information departments of colleges and universities. The jobs of these statisticians are nearly identical to that of the official team statistician for a professional team, in that they might record statistics in a manner similar to the one described above, but they might also be asked to do a lot of research and writing. Television stations often have a statistics and research staff responsible for collecting and verifying the statistics of any given sport. If the sport is fairly popular, they might assign someone to cover the events in that area, but if the sport is relatively young or not as popular, they might be asked to research information and statistics for that sport. The statistics and information are usually passed along to the sportscasters who are covering a game or event in that sport. Often, the statisticians are asked to write up notes for the sportscasters to use. For example, if the sportscasters are covering a baseball game, the statistician might come up with trivia or examples throughout the history of baseball when someone pitched no-hitters (a game where a pitcher does not allow an opposing team's batters to get a hit through nine innings or more of play) back-to-back.

Statisticians who work for private companies might be asked to keep statistics, field calls from sportswriters the day after a game about the stats for that game, or write notes up for one of their company's clients—notes regarding stats or trivia, for example.

Statisticians work both part time and full time, depending on the level of athletics in which they are involved, their degree of computer literacy and education, and whether they pursue freelance or full-time employment opportunities. The vast majority of individuals work part time, simply because they enjoy keeping stats for a team in a sport they love. Competition is incredibly fierce for full-time positions, whether for a sports information department at a college or university, a radio or television station or network sports show, or a private statistics company. Most statisticians advise students interested in entering the field to be persistent in asking for volunteer or part-time positions, to keep their schedules open in the event someone does call with a chance to score a game, and to be realistic about the chances of finding full-time work.

REQUIREMENTS

High School

Technically, there are no formal educational requirements for the job of sports statistician. Knowing how to manually score a game or event, and knowing as much as possible about the sport or sports for which you would like to keep statistics, are probably the only true requirements, but there are plenty of informal requirements that prospective sports statisticians should keep in mind.

First and foremost, although knowledge of manual scoring is essential, the future of sports statistics, like almost everything else, is tied to computers. The more you know about computers, from navigating your way around a keyboard to programming and troubleshooting, the better. Since most of the computer systems for the professional teams are privately owned, created expressly for the league or association, there isn't any way to study the programs used by professional teams while in high school or later. Becoming computer literate and having a working knowledge of common computer systems and programs, however, is the best way to ensure that, if necessary, you can pick up the intricacies of a new program after graduation.

Secondly, having a solid grasp of basic math skills is a necessity. To compute home run averages, you need to be able to figure averages. The formulas used to arrive at the different statistics are simple enough, but you must be good with math to figure them out yourself. On the job, you will probably use a calculator or computer, but if the computer system goes out you need to be able to do the math yourself. Take as many math classes as possible while in high school to build a strong foundation.

Good writing and communication skills are also vital to the statistician; you may find yourself trying to explain a statistic to a sportscaster or writer, or you may be asked to write notes concerning relevant statistics or trivia, even a press release. If you can't communicate information quickly and intelligently, you might find yourself out of a job. For this reason, take English literature and writing courses to develop your language skills while in high school.

Postsecondary Training
Private companies that employ sports statisticians will, however, most likely require candidates to have a bachelor's degree in statistics or in a related field, such as marketing, accounting, communications, or sports administration.

Other Requirements
To be a successful sports statistician, you need to be accurate, detail oriented, and thorough in your work. You should have good vision and be able to keep your concentration fully focused on the game at hand. Most importantly, you should enjoy athletics and competition. Many sports statisticians work part-time for reasons as simple as a love of the game.

EXPLORING

The best way to gain experience in this field is to learn as much as possible about how a sport is played and how to score it, especially those sports that you enjoy most. High school and college students can easily accomplish this by participating in sports or volunteering to act as statistician for one of the teams. If neither of these options is available, then simply by avidly attending games and scoring the various aspects of the game, whatever they may be, you can begin to pick up the finer points of scoring. In some sports, however, there are rather complicated statistics to score, such as earned-run averages in baseball.

There are books available for nearly every sport that explain, in detail, how to score particular statistics, but there is a better, more expedient way. Look around you at the next high school baseball or basketball game. Chances are a seasoned veteran of statistics is no less than two yards away. During a break or, better yet, after the game, introduce yourself and ask that person how to score a game. Most statisticians learned how to score sports events in precisely this way—by asking the people who have been doing it for years.

Another good reason for getting to know the professional scorers in this way is that one day they might need someone to cover a game, or know of an opening for a part-time statistician.

EMPLOYERS

Approximately 19,000 statisticians are employed in the United States, but sports statisticians make up only a very small portion of this group. Sports statisticians work for professional athletic teams, television and radio stations and networks, private companies, and college and university sports programs.

STARTING OUT

Many statisticians find part-time jobs when they are high school students and continue these jobs through college. Others go on to score stats for various teams at their college or university. The sports information departments at colleges and universities are also good places to look for part-time work. You might be assigned to the public relations office, in which case you would learn the related tasks, such as fielding calls from the media, writing press releases, and researching statistics for a specific team. Or, you might be assigned to work directly with a team as a statistician. In either case, many statisticians continue to volunteer or work part-time at stats jobs in order to maintain their scoring skills.

Television and radio stations are yet another way into the field of sports statistics. As mentioned, contacts are very helpful, but you can send your resume to the sports departments of various stations and channels, asking if they need another statistician. Be ready to volunteer if necessary or to work in the sometimes humbling position of a gofer. One longtime statistician advises prospective statisticians to be ready to score any game, anytime, anywhere, because one never knows which contact will eventually lead to something bigger and better. This also means being prepared to sacrifice personal time to a last-minute request from a statistician to cover a game in an emergency when he or she can't be there.

Finally, there are three companies that work with sports statistics: Elias Sports Bureau, PA Sport, and STATS. These companies employ statisticians and researchers to help provide clients (television, radio, and cable stations; magazines and newspapers) with sports statistics and research on a daily basis. These companies often offer internships and part-time jobs and are definitely one avenue to pursue for full-time jobs.

ADVANCEMENT

Part-time jobs keeping statistics for high school and college and university athletic teams can often lead to stats jobs with other organizations, including radio and television stations and private organizations, such as Elias Sports Bureau, PA Sport, and STATS. While not much of a hierarchy exists in these companies (most employees are either statisticians and researchers or executives), it is possible to advance to executive-level positions within these companies. While some people may leave these jobs to take others, most stay in these jobs for many years.

Statisticians who build solid reputations, who know the ins and outs of a particular sport, and who have excellent communication and math skills can often advance in the field to work for large radio and television networks.

EARNINGS

On the whole, competition will be keen for full-time jobs that offer competitive salaries in sports statistics. It is important to realize that many statisticians must work full-time jobs, often in totally unrelated fields, in order to support themselves. Only their love of the sport and statistics itself—and not the financial rewards of the jobs—keeps them involved with sports statistics.

Even for part-timers, much depends on the level of athletics in which the statistician is involved. For example, a statistician working freelance for a radio station covering the Memphis Grizzlies (an expansion professional basketball team) might receive $35 per game, whereas a statistician working freelance for one of the large television networks, such as FOX, might receive anywhere from $400 to $500 per game.

On the other hand, statisticians who work full-time for radio and television, or for companies like Elias Sports Bureau, receive salaries commensurate with jobs in other fields. An individual working with one of these companies for between one year and five years might earn $25,000 to $35,000 a year. If that person stayed with the company for another five to 10 years, he or she might earn between $35,000 and $50,000 a year. Statisticians who work for a company for many years can earn anywhere between $75,000 and $100,000 a year. Again, competition for these positions is extremely fierce.

In comparison to statisticians who work in the more traditional fields of statistical analysis, both in government and nongovernment jobs, sports statisticians with full-time positions have the opportunity to earn considerably higher salaries, although this may not always be the case. According to the U.S. Department of Labor, the median annual salary for statisticians was $65,720 in 2006. Salaries ranged from less than $37,010 to more than $108,630.

WORK ENVIRONMENT

Statisticians routinely work in the same conditions as do others in professions related to sports coverage, such as sportscasters, sportswriters, and sports agents. That is, they may spend time outdoors, in pleasant and inclement weather, but they also spend a lot of time indoors, in the media and statistics areas of sports stadiums and arenas, and in their own offices.

Statisticians also work odd hours, including weekends and holidays. In short, whenever there is a sports event scheduled that requires scorekeeping and statistics, one or more statisticians will be covering it. This can wreak havoc with the more nostalgic of holidays, such as Christmas and the Fourth of July; some football and many basketball games are scheduled on Christmas Eve and Christmas Day, while there are countless professional baseball games played on Independence Day.

OUTLOOK

As the impact of cable and satellite television enhances the marketability of the top five sports (football, baseball, basketball, hockey, and soccer), it will also bring into viewers' living rooms many sports not previously carried by the major networks. All of this increased sports coverage, plus developing technologies and markets on the Internet, will only increase the demand for sports statistics and the individuals who record and catalogue them. More importantly, perhaps, is the effect this new technology will have on those seeking jobs in sports statistics, as computer skills will become just as valuable to those interested in a career in sports statistics as in-depth knowledge of a sport. Those individuals who do have computer skills will be all the more marketable in the years to come. People already in the field will probably want to develop some degree of computer literacy.

On another note, even as the field develops, those currently with full-time positions in sports statistics aren't likely to leave those jobs. Attrition rates due to retirement and advancement, combined with the addition of some new positions, should keep this field developing about as fast as the average for all other occupations.

FOR MORE INFORMATION

For information on careers in statistics or schools that offer degrees in statistics, contact:
American Statistical Association
732 North Washington Street
Alexandria, VA 22314-1943
Tel: 888-231-3473
Email: asainfo@amstat.org
http://www.amstat.org

The following companies employ statisticians and researchers. Visit their Web sites for more information.
Elias Sports Bureau
http://www.esb.com

PA Sport
http://www.sportsticker.com

STATS
http://www.stats.com

Sports Trainers

QUICK FACTS

School Subjects
Health
Physical education

Personal Skills
Helping/teaching
Leadership/management

Work Environment
Indoors and outdoors
Primarily multiple locations

Minimum Education Level
Bachelor's degree

Salary Range
$21,940 to $36,560 to
$125,000

Certification or Licensing
Recommended

Outlook
Much faster than the average

DOT
153

GOE
14.08.01

NOC
4167

O*NET-SOC
29-9091.00

OVERVIEW

Sports trainers, also referred to as *athletic trainers*, *certified sports medicine trainers*, and *certified sports medicine therapists*, help amateur and professional athletes prevent injuries, give first aid when an injury occurs during a practice or event, and manage the rehabilitation programs and routines of injured athletes.

Athletic trainers often consult with physicians during all stages of athletic training to ensure that athletes under their care are physically capable of participating in competition. In addition, they specialize in health care administration, education, and counseling. There are approximately 15,000 athletic trainers employed in the United States.

HISTORY

Aristotle, Leonardo da Vinci, and Etienne Jules Marey all conducted experiments and studies involving motion and the human body, but it was the 19th-century French physiologist Marey whose devices to study human motion really advanced the field of biomechanics and sports medicine. In fact, both modern cinematography and sports medicine claim him as the father of their respective fields. Marey's first contribution was the first force platform, a device that was able to visualize the forces between the foot and the floor. Marey's pictures with the chronophotograph superimposed the stages of action onto a single photograph; in essence, giving form to motion and allowing scientists to study it frame by frame, motion by motion. By 1892, Marey had even made primitive motion pictures, but his cinematic efforts were quickly eclipsed by those of Louis and Auguste Lumiere.

Following both World Wars I and II, Marey's and other scientists' experiments with motion would combine with the need to heal and/or completely replace the limbs of war veterans. In order to provide an amputee with a prosthetic device that would come as close as possible to replicating the movement and functional value of a real limb, scientists and doctors began to work together to understand the range of motion and interrelationships peculiar to each part of the human body.

Mechanically, sports can be categorized according to the kinds of movements used. Each individual sport utilizes a unique combination of basic motions, including walking, running, jumping, kicking, and throwing. These basic motions have all been rigidly defined for scientific study so that injuries related to these motions can be better understood and treated. For example, sports that place heavy demands on one part of an athlete's body may overload that part and produce an injury, such as tennis elbow and swimmer's shoulder. Baseball, on the other hand, is a throwing sport, and certain injuries from overuse of the shoulder and elbow are expected. Athletes who play volleyball or golf also use some variation of the throwing motion and therefore sustain injuries to their shoulders and elbows.

Today, sports trainers are part of the team of sports medicine professionals that treat the injuries of both the amateur and elite athlete. Like sports physicians, certified sports trainers are responsible for preventing injuries as well as treating them, and they use their knowledge of the human body and its wide range of motions to discover new ways of reducing stress and damage from athletic activities. They work in high schools, secondary schools, colleges, and universities, and a smaller number work for professional teams. Many work in health clubs, sports medicine clinics, and other athletic health care settings. In 1990, the American Medical Association (AMA) recognized athletic training as an allied health profession.

THE JOB

Sports trainers help amateur and professional athletes prevent injuries through proper exercises and conditioning; provide immediate first-aid attention to injuries as they occur during a practice or event; and lead injured athletes safely through rehabilitation programs and routines. For the most part, sports trainers are not medical doctors, and are not allowed to conduct certain procedures or provide advanced types of medical care, such as prescribing or administering drugs. Some trainers, however, are trained physicians. If an individual is also trained as an *osteopathic physician*, for example, he or she is licensed as a medical doctor and can conduct more advanced procedures and techniques, including diagnosis, surgery, and the prescription of drugs.

In order to prevent injuries, sports trainers organize team physicals, making certain that each player is examined and evaluated by a physician prior to that athlete's participation in the sport. Along with the team physician, they help to analyze each athlete's overall readiness to play, fitness level, and known or existing weaknesses or injuries. When necessary, they recommend stretching, conditioning, and strengthening exercises to aid the athlete in preventing or exacerbating an injury. This may involve developing specific routines for individual athletes. Finally, athletic trainers work with coaches, and sometimes team physicians, to choose protective athletic equipment. Before games and practice, they often inspect the playing field, surface, or area for any flagrant or subtle risks of injury to the athlete.

Prior to a practice or competition, the athletic trainer may help an athlete conduct special stretching exercises or, as a preventive measure, he or she might tape, wrap, bandage, or brace knees, ankles, or other joints, and areas of the athlete's body that might be at risk for injury. The trainer routinely treats cuts, scratches, and abrasions, among other minor injuries. He or she may tape, pad, or wrap injuries, and install face guards. When serious injuries do occur, whether in practice or during a competition, the athletic trainer's role is to provide prompt and accurate first-aid treatment to the athlete to ensure that athlete's full recovery. He or she is trained in emergency procedures and is prepared to provide emergency treatment for conditions such as shock, concussion, or bone fracture, stabilizing the athlete until they reach a hospital or trauma center. Often, the trainer will accompany the injured athlete to the hospital, making certain the team physician is still on hand to address the health concerns and needs of those athletes who are still competing.

Working in concert with the team physician and several other health professionals, athletic trainers often supervise the therapeutic rehabilitation of athletes under their care. They analyze the athlete's injury and create individualized therapy routines. Sometimes, the trainer may advise the athlete to wear a protective brace or guard to minimize damage while the athlete is recuperating from an injury. Athletic trainers in charge of every level of athlete should be licensed to perform specific medical functions and operate certain devices and equipment.

REQUIREMENTS

High School

If you have an interest in becoming a sports trainer, you've probably already become involved in the field during high school. Maybe you're not an athlete but you work as a trainer or manager for one of your school teams. These are excellent ways to develop your interest in sports, learn about the skills that trainers must have, and develop the leadership abilities necessary for the job.

If you're interested in this field, you should pay special attention to physical education classes and to high school subjects such as health and anatomy and physiology. Students with an interest in becoming athletic trainers will want to become certified in CPR and first aid.

Postsecondary Training
Sports trainers usually earn a bachelor's degree from a college or university that offers a program in athletic training that is accredited by the Commission on Accreditation of Athletic Training Education (http://caate.net). Many students go on to earn a master's degree in athletic training. More than 70 percent of certified athletic trainers have at least a master's degree, according to the National Athletic Trainers' Association (NATA). Students then intern with a certified athletic trainer. Another option is to earn a bachelor's degree or a master's degree in a related health field, such as osteopathy, and then intern with a certified athletic trainer. The number of hours you need to spend in both clinical study and in the internship phase will vary, depending on the program you select and the professional organization that you decide to join.

Most accredited programs in athletic training include course work in the prevention and evaluation of athletic injuries and illnesses, first aid and emergency care, therapeutic exercises, therapeutic modalities, administration of athletic training programs, human anatomy, human physiology, exercise physiology, kinesiology, nutrition, psychology, and personal and community health.

Certification or Licensing
As mentioned earlier, athletic trainers in charge of every level of athlete should be licensed to perform specific medical functions and operate certain devices and equipment. Different membership organizations and their respective certifying bodies have different eligibility requirements; it is up to you to decide which organization best characterizes your ultimate goal.

For example, the NATA requires that each member have a bachelor's degree (in any field), be either a graduate of an accredited program in athletic training (with 800 clinical hours) or complete an internship (with 1,500 clinical hours), and pass a certification exam consisting of three sections—written, simulation, and oral practical.

Emerging Career Option:
Exercise Physiologist

Exercise is not just for the young and healthy. Today, it is prescribed as a way to help people recover from chronic illness, surgery, and injury. Exercise physiologists use their knowledge and training of exercise science to help patients reach optimum health, mobility, and confidence. Exercise physiologists work in clinical settings such as hospitals, nursing homes, and rehabilitation centers. They may also be employed by sports-related businesses such as health and fitness clubs or athletic training facilities and camps. Some choose to work in academia. A minimum of a bachelor's degree in exercise physiology or exercise science is required to enter this field, according to the American Society of Exercise Physiologists (http://www.asep.org), although a master's degree is usually a requirement for the best jobs. Salaries for exercise physiologists vary by type of employer, level of experience, and degree held. Exercise physiologists with a bachelor's degree earn $25,000 to $32,000; with a master's degree, $28,000 to $37,000; and with a doctorate, $30,000 to $60,000 or more.

Shane Paulson is an exercise physiologist and founder/CEO of PhysioLogic Human Performance Systems in Minnesota. He discussed his career with the editors of *Careers in Focus: Sports*.

Q. How long have you been an exercise physiologist? Tell us about your work background.
A. I have been an exercise physiologist for 10 years. I have worked in a couple of different settings. I've worked in a hospital cardiac rehabilitation program and worked for the military as an exercise physiologist. Currently, much of my work is with long-term care facilities to develop exercise physiology programs. Primarily, I am responsible for developing successful exercise physiology programs for organizations to help their clients and customers. The day-to-day

Approximately 43 states require some form of certification, licensure, or registration for athletic trainers. For more information, check with your state's regulatory agency in the state in which you would like to practice.

Other Requirements

Workers in this field need an understanding of human anatomy and physiology, both in terms of physical capabilities and injury treatment and prevention. You should not be squeamish when it comes to blood, broken bones, or other wounds. Athletes do get hurt, and a trainer who is unable to cope well with this aspect of sports may have a difficult time succeeding in the career. The ability and work involves a variety of different assessment techniques where results are used to prescribe safe, effective, and efficient exercise programs for individuals.

Q. What is one thing that young people may not know about a career in exercise physiology?
A. As one of the exercise sciences that have roots in sports medicine, there are obvious applications for the exercise physiologist in athletics and performance training situations, but many people don't know that exercise physiology is becoming a "new" healthcare profession. Disease prevention is becoming a main priority in government agencies and insurance providers, as well as with individuals. Exercise physiologists are working within the medical community to offer a new standard of care that is standardized and accountable.

Q. What are some of the pros and cons of your job?
A. I enjoy a great amount of respect for being very good at helping people. One of the harder aspects of my work is correcting the misinformation that people have come to believe about health and the popular pills and gadgets that have commercialized the fitness industry.

Q. How did you train for this job? What was your college major?
A. My undergraduate and graduate degrees are in exercise physiology, and I am a board certified exercise physiologist by the American Society of Exercise Physiologists (ASEP).

Q. What is the future employment outlook for exercise physiologists?
A. The future is full of opportunities for exercise physiologists. Students considering an exercise physiology career should attend an ASEP-accredited program and obtain board certification to best position themselves for those jobs.

knowledge to handle medical emergencies is especially important for certified athletic trainers, whose work focuses on injury prevention and treatment.

EXPLORING

Most trainers, like other professionals who work with athletes, were first drawn to sports as participants. High school and college students can gain valuable experience by actively participating in a sport. Such experience lends a prospective trainer added insight into the injuries typical of a given sport, as well as the compassion and empathy necessary to comfort an injured athlete who is forced to sit out a game. Most teams need help with everything from equipment to statistics, so plenty of opportunities exist to explore a variety of sports-related positions. If you are certain about becoming an athletic trainer, you can often work with and learn beside a trainer or team physician, learning beside a professional. This type of experience will come in handy later, when you are looking for an internship or a job; successful candidates are usually those with the most experience and on-the-job training.

EMPLOYERS

Approximately 15,000 athletic trainers are employed in the United States. Trainers are employed by professional and amateur sports teams, private sports organizations, sports facilities, educational institutions, and by individual athletes. Other possible athletic-training employment opportunities can be found in corporate health programs, health clubs, clinical and industrial health care programs, and athletic training curriculum programs.

STARTING OUT

Athletic trainers, regardless of the professional organization they join, are usually required to complete a period of training with a certified athletic trainer or sports medicine therapist. These internships provide students with the foundation for future networking possibilities. Many students find full-time jobs with the teams, organizations, or school districts with which they interned. At the very least, these internships offer students the chance to make valuable contacts and gain valuable on-the-job experience.

Most accredited programs in athletic training also have job placement departments that host recruitment seminars with major organizations, provide career counseling services, and put students in contact with prospective employers.

Finally, one of the benefits to belonging to a professional organization is that these associations publish newsletters and maintain Web sites, both of which list job openings. Some organizations even offer job hotlines to their members. Through these media, as well as through meetings, seminars, and continuing education, students and trainers can make new contacts that will help them locate work and add to their base of knowledge. NATA, for example, boasts the most comprehensive job referral service in the United States for athletic trainers, listing job openings in all athletic training settings and locations.

ADVANCEMENT

Acquiring additional training and education is the most common way of advancing in the field of sports training. Those trainers who have spent years working in the field and who update their skills each year by taking continuing education courses, sometimes even returning to school for an advanced degree, will be among the first to receive promotions.

Management responsibilities are the other way in which athletic trainers can advance in their field. Large universities often employ several trainers to serve the many different teams, with one trainer acting as the head trainer, sometimes also called the director of sports medicine. This individual coordinates the daily activities and responsibilities of the other trainers and works closely with the coaches of the school's various teams to ensure that all the demands are being met. Most often, trainers advance by working for several years at one school and then move on to another school when an opening is announced that will mean greater responsibilities and benefits.

EARNINGS

Earnings vary depending on the level of athletics in which the trainer is involved, the trainer's education and credentials, and the number and type of his or her responsibilities. Those considering a career as an athletic trainer should keep all aspects of the job and salary in perspective; the slight increase in salary of a trainer working for a college team might be offset by the higher stress levels and longer hours away from home. Trainers who work with professional athletes are away from home a great deal, including evenings, weekends, and holidays.

According to the National Association for Sport and Physical Education, salaries for athletic trainers in schools range from $25,000 to $35,000. With experience and a master's degree, college trainers can earn up to $45,000 to $60,000 per year. Athletic trainers who work for professional sports teams earn salaries ranging from $60,000 to $125,000.

The U.S. Department of Labor reports that athletic trainers earned median salaries of $36,560 in 2006. The highest 10 percent earned more than $57,580, while the lowest 10 percent earned less than $21,940.

WORK ENVIRONMENT

Athletes train year round and so do the sports trainers who supervise their conditioning and rehabilitation programs. Depending upon the level and size of an athletic program, trainers may work with athletes in one or more sports. Sports trainers who work in high schools often act as the trainer for several, or all, of the athletic teams. A lot also depends on the school's budgetary restrictions. Generally speaking, though, most schools have a separate trainer for men's and women's sports. Trainers in professional sports work only in one sport and for one team.

Most of the trainer's time is spent in the school's athletic facility, either in preparation for work or in conditioning or rehab sessions. Athletic trainers are on a schedule similar to that of their athletes; they go to practices, schedule weight and rehab sessions, and attend games. They are expected to travel when and where the team travels.

OUTLOOK

The U.S. Department of Labor predicts that athletic trainers will experience much faster than average job growth throughout 2014. The increasing number of amateur and school sports teams accounts for some of this growth, as does the public' increasing interest in health and fitness. Competition for the more glamorous jobs is tough; positions with professional athletes and teams are extremely difficult to find and those working in them usually have years and years of experience. More opportunities exist for certified athletic trainers who work with high school athletes, especially if trainers have other skills that make them more employable. For example, the athletic trainer wishing to work with high school athletes who also can teach biology, math, physical education, or other school subjects most likely will find a position sooner than the candidate with only a background in athletic training. The reasoning is simple: with school budgets being cut back, those individuals who perform double-duty will be more attractive to school boards looking to cut costs.

Positions at the college and university level offer the athletic trainer greater stability, with little turnover. Competition for these spots is also tough, however, and many schools are now requiring candidates to have a master's degree in order to be considered.

FOR MORE INFORMATION

To obtain publications about sports medicine, contact
American College of Sports Medicine
PO Box 1440
Indianapolis, IN 46206-1440
Tel: 317-637-9200
http://www.acsm.org

For information on certification, contact
Board of Certification Inc.
4223 South 143rd Circle
Omaha, NE 68137-4505
Tel: 877-262-3926
Email: staff@nataboc.org
http://www.bocatc.org

For a list of accredited athletic training programs, job listings, and information on certification, contact
National Athletic Trainers' Association
2952 Stemmons Freeway
Dallas, TX 75247-6916
Tel: 214-637-6282
http://www.nata.org

Sportswriters

QUICK FACTS

School Subjects
English
Journalism
Physical education

Personal Skills
Communication/ideas

Work Environment
Indoors and outdoors
Primarily multiple locations

Minimum Education Level
Bachelor's degree

Salary Range
$25,430 to $48,640 to
$97,700+

Certification or Licensing
None available

Outlook
About as fast as the average

DOT
131

GOE
01.02.01

NOC
5231

O*NET-SOC
27-3043.02

OVERVIEW

Sportswriters cover the news in sports for newspapers and magazines. They research original ideas or follow up on breaking stories, contacting coaches, athletes, and team owners and managers for comments or more information. Sometimes a sportswriter is fortunate enough to get his or her own column, in which the sportswriter editorializes on current news or developments in sports.

HISTORY

Throughout the world there are some 7,200 daily newspapers and far more semiweeklies, biweeklies, and weeklies, circulating at least 500 million copies on a regular basis. In the international context, the average newspaper is crude, poorly printed, heavy with sensational news, light on serious criticism, and burdened by all types of problems (especially economic). Outside Western Europe and North America there are very few "elite," or ultra-serious, newspapers. Although most of the world's newspapers are privately owned, some degree of government control is evident in many countries.

Magazine journalism has been a potent force in the United States (and throughout the world), appealing mainly to the elite, the well-educated, and opinion leaders. At least this is true in the sense of "journalistic" magazines. Generally more incisive, more articulate, more interpretive, and certainly more comprehensive than newspapers, magazines have supplied an important intellectual dimension to news-oriented journalism. Whereas the main function of newspaper journalism is to inform or summarize in brief fashion, the aim of most magazine journalism is to fill gaps—to explain, interpret, criticize, and comment. In short, magazine journalism in its many types and styles supplements newspapers and fleshes out the bare bones of newspaper journalism.

Most magazines and newspapers have sections that focus on sports; others, such as *Sports Illustrated* and *ESPN The Magazine*, focus entirely on sports reporting. In either case, sportswriters are needed to write articles about athletes, teams, and sports competitions. Sportswriters are employed by both newspapers and magazines throughout the United States.

THE JOB

The sportswriter's primary job is to report the outcomes of the sports events that occurred that day. Since one newspaper can't employ enough reporters to cover, in person, every single high school, college, and professional sports event that happens on any given day, let alone sports events happening in other cities and countries, sportswriters use the wire news services to get the details. Major national and international wire services include Reuters, AP, UPI, Agence France-Presse, and ITAR-Tass. The entire body of statistics for tennis matches, hockey games, and track-and-field events, for example, can be sent over the wire service so that sportswriters can include the general story and the vital statistics in as condensed or lengthy a form as space allows.

A sportswriter begins work each day by reviewing the local, national, and international news that comes in over the wire news services. He or she then begins researching the top or lead stories to try to flesh out the story, perhaps with a local perspective on it. An example of a lead story might be the comeback of a professional tennis star; the underdog victory of a third-rate, much-maligned football team; the incredible pitching record of a high school athlete; or the details of a football running back who blew out his knee in a crucial last-minute play. The sportswriter then calls or interviews in person coaches, athletes, scouts, agents, promoters, and sometimes, in the case of an athletic injury, a physician or team of physicians.

Depending on the edition of the newspaper or magazine, the sportswriter might report events that happened anywhere from the day before to events that took place within that week or month. For example, a sportswriter who writes for a magazine such as *Sports Illustrated* probably won't write articles with the same degree of detail per game. Instead, he or she writes articles, commonly called features that explore an entire season for a team or an athlete. The magazine sportswriter might take the same story of the running back with the damaged knee ligaments and follow that athlete through his

Sportswriters interview David Stern, commissioner of the National Basketball Association, before a game. *(Frank Polich, Reuters, Corbis)*

surgery and rehabilitation, interviewing the running back as well as his wife, doctors, coaches, and agent. This stage of gathering information is the same for both newspaper and magazine sportswriters, the only difference is the time line. A newspaper sportswriter may have only a few hours to conduct research and call around for comments, while the sportswriter for a magazine may have anywhere from several weeks to several months to compose the story.

Regardless of whether the sportswriter works for a newspaper or magazine, the next step for the sportswriter is to write the story. The method will vary, again, depending on the medium. Most sportswriters for newspapers are subject to the constraints of space, and these limits can change in a matter of minutes. On a dull day, up until the hour before the paper is published, the sportswriter might have a quarter of a page to fill with local sports news. At the last minute, however, an entire Super Bowl team could come down with food poisoning, in which case the sports editor would probably want to cover this larger, breaking story. To accommodate the new articles about the poisoning, the effect on team morale, whether or not the Super Bowl might be postponed for the first time in history, the local sports coverage would either have to shrink considerably or be completely cut. To maintain this required flexibility, sportswriters, like other reporters who write for daily newspapers, compose their stories with the most crucial facts contained within the first one or two paragraphs of the story. They may write a 10-paragraph story, but if it had to be shortened, the pertinent information would be easily retained.

Sportswriters for magazines, on the other hand, seldom need to worry about their stories being cut down at the last minute. Rather, their stories are subject to more careful editing. Magazines usually have story meetings weeks or months in advance of the relevant issue, giving sportswriters ample time to plan, research, and write their articles. As a result of the different timetable, the presentation of the story will change. The sportswriter will not cram all the essential facts into an opening paragraph or two. Instead, he or she is allowed much greater leeway with the introduction and the rest of the article. The sportswriter, in this case, will want to set a mood in the introduction, developing the characters of the individuals being interviewed—literally, telling a story about the story. In short, details can hinder a newspaper sports story from accomplishing its goal of getting across the facts in a concise form, while in a magazine sports article, those extraneous, revealing details actually become part of the story.

Even with the help of news services, sportswriters still couldn't have all the sports news at their fingertips without the help of other reporters and writers, known in the world of reporting as *stringers*. A stringer covers an event that most likely would not be covered by the wire services, events such as high school sports events, as well as games in professional sports that are occurring simultaneously with other major sports events. The stringer attends the sports event and phones in scores, or emails or faxes in a complete report.

While the sportswriters for magazines don't necessarily specialize in one area of sports, but instead, routinely write features on a wide variety of sports and athletes, sportswriters for newspapers do specialize. Many only cover a particular sport, such as baseball. Others are assigned a beat, or specific area, and like other reporters must cover all the events that fall into that beat. For example, a sportswriter assigned to the high school football beat for a newspaper in Los Angeles, California, would be expected to cover all area high school football games. Since football is seasonal, he or she might be assigned to the high school basketball beat during the winter season. On the other hand, a sportswriter working in Lexington, Kentucky, might be assigned coverage of all the high school sports in the area, not simply one sport. Much of the way in which assignments are given depends on experience as well as budget and staffing constraints.

REQUIREMENTS

High School

English, journalism, and speech are the most important classes for you to take in high school. You will need to master the art of writing in order to convey your ideas concisely, yet creatively, to your readers. Speech classes will help you become comfortable interacting with others. Be sure to take physical education classes and participate in organized sports, be it as a competitor, a team manager, or an assistant. You also should join the staff of your school paper or yearbook. This will give you a chance to cover and write about your school's sports teams or other school activities.

Postsecondary Training

You will need at least a bachelor's degree to become a sportswriter, although many sportswriters go on to study journalism at the graduate level. Most sportswriters concentrate on journalism while in college, either by attending a program in journalism or by taking whatever courses are available outside of a specialized program. This isn't to say that you can't become a sportswriter without a degree in journalism, but competition for sportswriting jobs is incredibly fierce. After all, sportswriters get great seats at sports events, and they have the credentials to get them into interviews with sports celebrities. Increasingly, a specialized education is becoming the means by which sports editors and managers sift through the stacks of resumes from prospective sportswriters. Sportswriters may have degrees in communications or English, among other majors.

Other Requirements

Clearly, the ability to write well and concisely is another requirement for the job of the sportswriter. In addition, you must have a solid understanding of the rules and play of many different sports. If you hope to specialize in the coverage of one particular sport, your knowledge of that sport has to be equal to that of anyone coaching or playing it at the professional level.

Finally, you must be able to elicit information from a variety of sources, as well as to determine when information being leaked is closer to promotional spin than to fact. There will be more times when a coach or agent will not want to comment on a story than the times when they will want to make an on-the-record comment, so the sportswriter must be assertive in pressing the source for more information.

EXPLORING

You can learn on-the-job skills by working for your high school and college papers. The experience can be related to sports, of course, but any journalistic experience will help you develop the basic skills useful to any reporter, regardless of the area about which you are writing.

You can increase your chances and success in the field by applying to colleges or universities with renowned academic programs in journalism. Most accredited programs have a required period of training in which you will intern with a major newspaper somewhere in the United States; student-interns are responsible for covering a beat.

Books to Read

Aamidor, Abraham. *Real Sports Reporting.* Bloomington, Ind.: Indiana University Press, 2003.

Andrews, Phil. *Sports Journalism: A Practical Introduction.* Thousand Oaks, Calif.: Sage Publications Ltd., 2005.

Eskenazi, Gerald. *A Sportswriter's Life: From the Desk of a New York Times Reporter.* Columbia, Mo.: University of Missouri Press, 2004.

Maraniss, David, and Glenn Stout, eds. *The Best American Sports Writing 2007.* Boston: Houghton Mifflin, 2007.

Sporting News. *All American Sports IQ Test: Ultimate Playbook of Trivia, Teasers and Puzzles.* New York: Sporting News Books, 2004.

Staten, Vince. *Why Is The Foul Pole Fair?: Answers to 101 of the Most Perplexing Baseball Questions.* New York: Simon & Schuster, 2004.

Walsh, Christopher J. *No Time Outs: What It's Really Like to Be a Sportswriter Today.* Lanham, Md.: Taylor Trade Publishing, 2006.

Wilstein, Steve. *Associated Press Sports Writing Handbook.* New York: McGraw-Hill, 2001.

You may also find it helpful to read the sports section of your local newspaper or other publications that are related to this field, such as *Sports Illustrated* (http://www.si.com) and *Sports Business Journal* (http://www.sportsbusinessjournal.com), and visit Web sites such as the Associated Press Sports Editors (http://apse.dallasnews.com).

EMPLOYERS

Sportswriters are employed by newspapers, magazines, and Web sites throughout the world. They may cover professional teams based in large cities or high school teams located in tiny towns. Sportswriters also work as freelance writers.

STARTING OUT

You may have to begin your career as a sportswriter by covering the games or matches that no else wants to or can cover. As a stringer, you won't earn much money, you'll probably have a second or even third job, but eventually it may lead to covering bigger and better games and teams. Some sportswriters make a living out of covering sports for very small towns; others only work at those jobs until they have gained the experience to move on.

Most journalists start their careers by working in small markets—little towns and cities with local papers. You may work for a newspaper for a year or two and then apply for positions with larger papers in bigger towns and cities. Sportswriters for newspapers follow the same routine, and more than a few end up pursuing areas other than sports because the job openings in sports simply weren't there. The lucky few who hang on to a small sports beat can often parlay that beat into a better position by sticking with the job and demonstrating a devotion to the sport, even cultivating a following of loyal fans. This could lead to a full-time column.

Most likely, as a sportswriter, you will take advantage of opportunities to learn more about athletes and sports in general. Becoming an expert on a little-known but rapidly growing sport may be one way for you to do this. For example, if you were to learn all that you can about mountain biking, you might be able to land a job with a magazine specializing in the sport.

Competition for full-time jobs with magazines as a sportswriter is just as keen as it is for major newspapers. Often a sportswriter will write articles and try to sell them to one of the major magazines, hoping that when an opening comes, he or she will have first crack at it. Still, most sportswriters move into the world of sports magazines after they've proven themselves in newspaper sportswriting. It is possible, however, to get a job with a sports magazine straight from college or graduate school; chances are you'll have to work your way up, though.

The placement centers of colleges or universities with accredited undergraduate and graduate programs in journalism can be extremely helpful in beginning your job search. In fact, many graduates of these programs are not only highly sought after by newspapers and magazines, but these graduates are often offered jobs by the newspapers and magazines with whom they had an internship during school.

ADVANCEMENT

The constraints of budget, staffing, and time—which make a sportswriters' job difficult—are also often what can help a sportswriter rise through the ranks. For example, the writer asked to cover all the sports in a small area may have to hustle to cover the beat alone, but that writer also won't have any competition when covering the big events. Thus, he or she can gain valuable experience and bylines writing for a small paper, whereas in a larger market, the same sportswriter would have to wait much longer to be assigned an event that might result in a coveted byline.

Sportswriters advance by gaining the top assignments, covering the major sports in feature articles, as opposed to the bare bones summaries of events. They also advance by moving to larger and larger papers, by getting columns, and finally, by getting a syndicated column—that is, a column carried by many papers around the country or even around the world.

Sportswriters for magazines advance by moving up the publishing ladder, from *editorial assistant* to *associate editor* to *writer*. Often, an editorial assistant might be assigned to research a story for a sports brief—a quirky or short look at an element of the game. For example, *Sports Illustrated* might have a page devoted to new advances in sports equipment for the amateur athlete. The editorial assistant might be given the idea and asked to research it, or specific items. A writer might eventually write it up, using the editorial assistant's notes. Advancement, then, comes in being actually listed as the author of the piece.

In the publishing worlds of both newspapers and magazines, sportswriters can advance by becoming editors of a newspaper's sports page or of a sports magazine. There are also sports publicists and sports information directors who work for the publicity and promotions arms of colleges, universities, and professional sports teams. These individuals release statements, write and disseminate to the press articles on the organizations' teams and athletes, and arrange press opportunities for coaches and athletes.

EARNINGS

According the U.S. Department of Labor, writers employed in all industries had median annual earnings of $48,640 in 2006. The lowest 10 percent earned less than $25,430, while the highest 10 percent earned more than $97,700. Sportswriters who cover major sports events, who have their own column, or who have a syndicated column can expect to earn more than the salaries above. Sportswriters who write for major magazines can also expect to earn more, sometimes per article, depending on their reputations and the contracts worked out by themselves or their agents.

WORK ENVIRONMENT

Like other journalists, sportswriters work in a variety of conditions, from the air-conditioned offices of a newsroom or magazine publisher to the sweaty, humid locker room of a professional basketball team, to the arid and dusty field where a baseball team's spring training is held. Sportswriters work irregular hours, putting in as much or as little time as the story requires, often traveling to small towns and out-of-the-way locales to cover a team's away games.

The benefits are obvious: For the individuals who love sports, the job offers the chance to cover sports events every day, to immerse themselves in the statistics and injury lists and bidding wars of professional and amateur sports, and to speak, sometimes one-on-one, with talented athletes.

OUTLOOK

The turnover rate for top sportswriters with major newspapers and magazines isn't very high, which means that job openings occur as sportswriters retire, die, are fired, or move into other markets. While the publishing industry may have room in it for yet another magazine devoted to a particular sports specialty, competition for sportswriting jobs will continue to be strong into 2014 and beyond.

FOR MORE INFORMATION

Associated Press Sports Editors is a membership organization that strives to improve print journalistic standards in sports newsrooms. Web site visitors will find up-to-date news articles regarding industry happenings, a job board, and a downloadable monthly newsletter, as well as links to Web sites for all of the major professional sports organizations and leagues. Membership information, including an in-depth profile of the organization, is also included.

Associated Press Sports Editors
c/o The Dallas Morning News: Sports Day
508 Young Street
Dallas, TX 75202-4808
Tel: 214-977-8222
http://apse.dallasnews.com

The AWSM is a membership organization of women and men employed in sports writing, editing, broadcast and production, public relations, and sports information. Visit its Web site for information on internships and scholarships.

Association for Women in Sports Media (AWSM)
PO Box F
Bayville, NJ 08721-0317
http://www.awsmonline.org

Founded in 1958 by the Wall Street Journal *to improve the quality of journalism education, this organization offers internships, scholarships, and literature for college students. To read* The Journalist's Road to Success: A Career Guide, *which lists schools*

offering degrees in news-editing, and financial aid to those inter-
ested in print journalism, visit the DJNF Web site:
  Dow Jones Newspaper Fund (DJNF)
  PO Box 300
  Princeton, NJ 08543-0300
  Tel: 609-452-2820
  Email: newsfund@wsj.dowjones.com
  http://djnewspaperfund.dowjones.com

For information on careers, contact
  Football Writers Association of America
  http://www.sportswriters.net/fwaa

Career information, including a pamphlet called Facts about Newspapers, *is available from*
  Newspaper Association of America
  4401 Wilson Boulevard, Suite 900
  Arlington, VA 22203-1867
  Tel: 571-366-1000
  http://www.naa.org

For information on careers and salaries in the newspaper industry,
contact
  The Newspaper Guild-CWA (Communications Workers of
    America)
  501 Third Street, NW, Suite 250
  Washington, DC 20001-2797
  Tel: 202-434-7177
  Email: guild@cwa-union.org
  http://www.newsguild.org

INTERVIEW

Tom Shatel, a sportswriter at the Omaha World-Herald *(http://*
www.omaha.com) in Omaha, Nebraska, discussed his career with
the editors of Careers in Focus: Sports.

Q. How did you get your first job in this field? What did you do?

A. My first job was as a preps writer at the *Kansas City Star* in August, 1980, three months after I graduated from the University of Missouri. I had worked for the *Star* as a campus correspondent my senior year at Mizzou, doing sidebars and assorted legwork, women's games, features, etc. A job opened up and I was at the right place at the right time. Most of my Mizzou colleagues began their careers in small towns before moving up.

Q. What are some of the pros and cons of your job?

A. The pros are that I get to be a sportswriter, do what I love, and do what I've always wanted to do, which is attend sporting events and be around the people who play and coach the games and write about them, tell their stories. The cons are travel, I hate traveling now, and the discord between writers and coaches and players. Coaches use talk radio and bloggers as an excuse to not say anything and give less access. I miss eating and drinking with coaches after games, getting to know their families, hanging out in their offices. You can do those things and still be critical of them. Those are the relationships you live for.

Q. What are the most important personal and professional qualities for sportswriters?

A. Make sources, get out and get around to know people on your beat, and be fair and trustworthy. Don't burn a source to get a story; I've yet to find a case where that was worth it. Don't take personal shots at someone just to be funny. A writer who is in the Baseball Hall of Fame once told me, let the facts speak for themselves. Good advice, I think.

Q. What are the key elements of a well-written column?

A. I think the best columns tell you something you didn't know, which requires reporting, makes you think, and makes you feel. Those are the ones I always remember—and get feedback from. Not every column can be that way. You can't force emotion or create a story that's not there. But those things should be the goal.

Q. What advice would you give to young people who are interested in the field?

A. Go into law or medicine. Just kidding. It's a worthwhile venture, but it's a tough business now. Papers are cutting staff, not adding. I would say be handy with a computer and/or video camera. More and more writers are going to have to do video feeds for their online editions in the future. Mostly, work harder than your competition, get plenty of clips, and don't give up. Like I said, it's tough out there.

Stadium Ushers and Vendors

OVERVIEW

Stadium ushers take tickets, escort spectators to their seats, and provide spectators with information and direction upon request.

Stadium vendors sell a variety of food items and other wares either by walking around and calling out the name of the food or product they are selling, or by operating small booths or kiosks. Sometimes vendors are hired by the food service franchise that is licensed to sell food in a stadium or sports facility.

HISTORY

As long as people have been gathering in places such as theaters or sporting events, there has been a need for crowd control. Ushers direct the audience or spectators to their seats, take care of complaints, and keep order among enthusiastic spectators. Whether in a Roman amphitheater or at a modern domed stadium, ushers have been present to help people find their seats. In ancient times, it was customary among Roman dignitaries to have a servant called an *ustiarius*, from which the word usher is derived, standing at the door to announce the arrival of their guests. Vendors have an ancient tradition as well. The Latin word *vendre* literally means to sell. A stadium vendor is an independent, licensed operator selling to the stadium crowds.

THE JOB

The work of stadium ushers and vendors varies with the place, the event, and the audience, but their duties while working sports events

QUICK FACTS

School Subjects
Business
Speech

Personal Skills
Following instructions
Leadership/management

Work Environment
Indoors and outdoors
Primarily one location

Minimum Education Level
High school diploma

Salary Range
$12,168 to $15,880 to
$24,340+

Certification or Licensing
None available

Outlook
About as fast as the average

DOT
344

GOE
11.02.01

NOC
6213, 6683

O*NET-SOC
39-3031.00

are similar. The main job of the usher is to seat patrons. Other duties for the usher might include finding empty available seats for patrons, locating lost items, helping children find their parents, paging people, checking and recording thermometer readings, answering questions, giving directions, attempting to control unruly or ill-behaved people, and settling arguments about seat assignments. In the event that spectators grow unreasonably unruly or out-of-control, it is the responsibility of ushers to notify security of the disturbance. Ushers watch exits and show patrons to restrooms, drinking fountains, and telephones. They keep aisles clear of objects that might cause patrons to slip or fall.

Similarly, a vendor sells food and other items at a variety of sports events, although the amounts and items sold might vary depending on the event. For example, a vendor selling beer would probably sell more beers during a hockey or football game than during a figure-skating competition; in many cases, they might not even sell beer at such competitions. The vendor may be either an independent seller, licensed by the local government to sell his or her wares, or a vendor working as a freelance operator under license by the owner of the site. For example, the manager of the sports facility allows freelance operators to sell hot dogs, sodas, ice cream and all the other foods and services enjoyed during a ball game. Or a vendor might be employed by the franchise licensed to sell T-shirts, caps, and other sports paraphernalia at sports events.

Food vendors are often responsible for preparing the food for sale (and sometimes this just means placing a hot dog inside a bun), as well as handling the sale, making change, and providing any additional items necessary to the consumption of the food, such as napkins, straws, and condiments.

REQUIREMENTS
High School
High school students fill many of the usher and vendor positions in theaters and stadiums, although there is an age requirement for vendors who sell alcoholic beverages. Good standing in high school or a high school diploma is usually required. Employers will strongly consider your school attendance record, so regular and prompt attendance is advised.

Postsecondary Training
Vendors and ushers are not required to have college-level education or training. Most training is conducted on the job for a brief time and new employees are used to fill the less responsible jobs and quieter locations. While the trainees are learning, they are shifted to different parts of the stadium as the need arises.

Certification or Licensing

Although ushers and vendors are not required to be certified, those who sell alcohol or certain other items must have a license.

Other Requirements

To be a successful stadium usher or vendor, you need to be affable and friendly. You should have strong oral communication skills in order to interact successfully with the general public. Strong mathematical skills will help you deal with the transfer of money. You should be physically fit because you will be on your feet during much of your shift. Finally, you should be willing to work outdoors in sometimes harsh weather conditions, such as extreme cold or heat, driving rain, sleet, or snow.

EXPLORING

Labor unions represent many ushers in stage production theaters, ballparks, and sports arenas and usually welcome the opportunity to talk with young people about working as an usher or vendor. Another option is to call the ballpark or stadium directly to find out more about being an usher or vendor. When you learn of special events coming to your town, contact the coordinator and volunteer your services to get a taste for the job.

Although these jobs are not the most glamorous, they will give you a chance to learn about sport facility management and concessions, experience which may come in handy later if you are serious about exploring either career option.

EMPLOYERS

Ushers are employed anywhere that a large group of people gather to watch some type of event or show. Movie theaters, sports stadiums, and colleges/universities are the largest employers of ushers.

Vendors are also employed wherever large groups of people gather to view an event or a show, but with one small difference. During these events, the people must have the time and the ability to spend money on food, drink, and souvenirs. For example, while a cotton candy vendor is right at home at the circus or ballpark, he or she might stick out like a sore thumb at the opera.

STARTING OUT

Check with theaters, ballparks, convention centers, and colleges in your area and inquire about possible openings. There is a lot of turnover in this business, so openings are usually plentiful but are snatched up quickly.

Positions in stadiums are usually part time and seasonal; jobs as ushers or vendors in a stadium used only for baseball end in the fall; if the stadium is domed, there might be additional opportunities to usher or vend during concerts or conventions. Depending on whether or not the vendor is independent or employed by a food or clothing franchise, the vendor may have opportunities year-round. Also, the contacts one makes in these jobs can lead to better jobs in the future.

ADVANCEMENT

Those stadium ushers or vendors with the most experience usually receive the positions with greater responsibilities, such as handling emergency evacuation procedures. Frequently, ushers and vendors work in crews of three or more, with one individual acting as the supervisor for that crew or team.

In addition to advancing within the categories of ushers and vendors, individuals who have interests in other areas of the game—from public relations to marketing—can make contacts with people who work full time in those areas and possibly arrange an internship or part-time job. Many people who now work for major sports franchises in a variety of front-office jobs once spent a summer working as a stadium usher or vendor.

EARNINGS

Three-fourths of all stadium ushers and vendors work part time or seasonally. The range of weekly hours is from 20 to 50 hours.

Hourly rates vary from job to job. Most ushers work at their job for such a short time that they seldom earn more than the starting wage. Hourly wages ranged from minimum wage to more than $11.70 an hour in 2006, according to the U.S. Department of Labor. The median hourly pay was $7.64 in 2006, which translates into $15,880 a year for full-time work. The pay rate has increased somewhat due to the demand for this type of worker in most cities. Experienced ushers in metropolitan areas earn the highest wages. For vendors, the amount earned is usually on a commission basis and the competition can be fierce to get the most desired concessions in the park (hot dogs, ice cream, and so on).

For many ushers and vendors, the real reward in working these jobs comes from the chance to be a part of a large-scale event, such as a baseball or football game, where they can be an integral part of the production of the event as well as enjoy the sport.

WORK ENVIRONMENT

Stadium ushers and vendors working in domed stadiums or indoor arenas or other indoor sports facilities don't have to brave the elements, while ushers and vendors who work football games need to dress warmly, as they frequently work in cold, sometimes miserable conditions. Ushers spend most of their working time standing or walking up and down aisles. In stadiums, ushers and vendors may do considerable climbing up and down stairs or tiers to seat patrons. Work can be stressful when patrons complain or when a crowd gets out of hand.

OUTLOOK

Stadium revenue rises and falls with the success and failure of the home team; if the team is doing well, crowds swell and fill the stands. Jobs will always exist for ushers and vendors in sports facilities, and these skills are applicable to other venues that use ushers and vendors, such as music halls and theaters.

Turnover in this work is high. Most openings arise as people leave the field for different reasons. Many leave to take better paying jobs. Students working part time usually leave when they graduate from high school or college.

FOR MORE INFORMATION

In addition to the following organization, individuals interested in pursuing a job as an usher or vendor should contact the sports facilities in their area, from colleges to universities to professional teams, to ask about job openings.

For information about major convention and assembly management companies, contact
International Association of Assembly Managers
635 Fritz Drive, Suite 100
Coppell, TX 75019-4442
Tel: 972-906-7441
http://www.iaam.org

For industry information, contact
Stadium Managers Association
525 SW 5th Street, Suite A
Des Moines, IA 50309-4501
Tel: 515-282-8192
http://www.stadiummanagers.org

Umpires and Referees

OVERVIEW

Umpires and *referees* ensure that competitors in athletic events follow the rules. They make binding decisions and have the power to impose penalties upon individuals or teams that break the rules. Umpires, referees, and other sports officials hold about 16,000 jobs in the United States.

HISTORY

The history of sport goes back to the time of the ancient Olympic games, ritualistic ball games of Central and South America, and gladiator battles of Rome. Since gladiator battles were fights to the death, there were no rules to be observed and no need for umpires or referees to ensure fairness.

As athletics became more organized, if not less violent, rules were established, and umpires and referees were needed to enforce these rules and regulations. Boxing, soccer, and rugby were the first sports to have trained officials. With the advent of professional sports such as baseball and basketball, officiating became a career option.

THE JOB

Every sport has its own set of rules and regulations. Even the same game played on different levels may have its own distinct rules. For example, in professional basketball, the team in possession of the ball has 24 seconds to take a shot on goal. On the college level, the shot clock is set at 35 seconds for men's competition and 30 seconds for women's competition, and in the game played by most high school teams, there is no shot clock at all.

Sports officials are the experts on the playing field. They know all the rules for the sport they officiate. They observe players while the ball or puck is in play and penalize those who break the rules. They are the decision makers and the arbiters of disputes between the competing teams.

When an official spots an infraction of the rules, he or she blows a whistle to stop play. The penalty is communicated to the official scorer, the penalty is assessed, and play continues.

Major League Baseball utilizes four *umpires* for each game. The *home plate umpire* works behind home plate and is responsible for determining whether each pitched ball is thrown within the strike zone. The home plate umpire also rules whether runners crossing home plate are safe or out and keeps track of the ball/strike count on each batter.

Other umpires are responsible for the three bases. They decide whether runners are safe or out at their respective bases. *First- and third-base umpires* also must observe whether a ball, batted to the outfield, lands on the playing field within the foul line.

It is not uncommon for a single official to work a Little League game. When this is the case, the umpire stands behind the plate. The umpire is responsible for calling balls and strikes, keeping track of the number of outs and the ball/strike count, watching the foul line, and ruling on runners at the bases.

Three officials work National Basketball Association games. They are more active than baseball umpires. *Basketball referees* run up and down the court, following both the ball and the players. They must not only watch the ball, but must keep an eye out for illegal contact between players.

If three officials are supervising the game, one stands near the basket of the offensive team, another stands at the free throw line extended, and the third stands on the opposite side of the court (from the second official) halfway between mid-court and the free throw line. Each official watches different parts of the court for infractions. For instance, the official near the basket makes sure that no offensive player stands inside the free throw lane for more than three seconds.

High school and college games have two or three officials. Grade school and amateur league games generally have two. Again, the rules may be slightly different, and the athletic ability may vary, but the game is still basketball.

Football games use between four and seven officials. Like other referees, *football officials* each have specific areas to observe. The referee, who is ultimately in charge, is positioned behind the offensive team.

An umpire calls a base runner safe during a Major League Baseball game. *(Paul Buck, epa, Corbis)*

Football referees are responsible for watching the offensive backfield for illegal movement before the ball is put into play, and they also communicate all penalties to the coaches and official scorer.

Another official observes the line of scrimmage for offsides penalties and marks the progress of the ball. The football umpire stands on the defensive team's side, five yards off the line of scrimmage, and watches for illegal blocks in the line. Other officials stand in the defensive backfield and observe defenders and receivers for illegal contact or interference.

Hockey games have three officials who skate up and down the ice. The *hockey referee*, who is in charge, stands between the other hockey umpires and assesses penalties. The linesmen call offsides and icing violations. Off the ice, the *penalty time keeper* keeps track of penalty time served, and two *goal judges* determine whether shots on goal have eluded the goalie and entered the net.

REQUIREMENTS

High School
If you are interested in becoming a sports official, you should begin learning as much as you can about sports and their rules. You will also want to get in the physical shape necessary to keep up with the athletes during an event. The best way to accomplish these goals is to participate in school sports.

In class, you will want to focus on English grammar and also other languages if you are interested in working as a baseball umpire or hockey official. Speech, debate, or theater courses will build your self-confidence and teach you the diction skills you need to be understood clearly.

Finally, sports bring together many kinds of people, and as an umpire or referee you must be diplomatic with all of them. Classes in sociology, history, and psychology can help you learn about the different cultures and ways of thinking of people from all parts of the world.

Postsecondary Training

While umpires and referees are not required to attend four-year colleges or universities, many do have college degrees. Often sports officials are former college athletes who decided to pursue a career in sports in a nonperformance capacity. Obviously, attending college and participating in college athletics is an excellent way to reinforce your knowledge of a sport and its rules while receiving a solid education.

The International Association of Approved Basketball Officials has schools that run each summer in different places in the United States. There, referees learn rules and work games at the players' camps that are held in conjunction with the schools. Officials for the National Football League must meet the requirements that enable them to become accredited association of football officials.

In almost all cases, officials must attend special training schools or courses. These can vary from the two schools (the Jim Evans Academy of Professional Umpiring and the Harry Wendelstedt School for Umpires) endorsed by Major League Baseball's Umpire Development Program all the way to the training courses offered to officials in amateur softball. These schools and training courses can be contacted through professional and amateur leagues, college athletic conferences, and state interscholastic commissions. These organizations can also inform you of minimum age requirements (usually 18 and out of high school) and other criteria that vary between leagues and sports.

Certification or Licensing

The special training programs that umpires and referees attend act as their certification. Without these, they are not eligible to officiate. These courses may vary, ranging from those in the official training schools of professional umpires to courses taken through a state interscholastic athletic commission for middle school volleyball officials.

Facts About Professional Baseball Umpires

- There are 70 umpires working in 17 crews of four (with two national rovers) at the major league level.
- Most umpires spend eight to 12 years in the minor leagues before being promoted to the major leagues. There is typically one opening at the major league level per year.
- Major league umpires earn starting salaries of about $120,000. The most experienced umpires earn up to $350,000.
- Major league umpires receive a daily allowance of $340, which covers hotels, rental car, tips, meals, and other incidentals.

Source: Major League Baseball

Other Requirements

Different sports have different physical requirements. For example, to be a hockey official, you need be an accomplished skater and should be in excellent health. General physical requirements include good vision, to some extent good hearing, and good physical health.

Sports officials must have good communication skills and the ability to make split-second decisions. Many calls that an official makes will be unpopular, so you will need courage to make the correct call and confidence to stand behind your judgment. An easily intimidated official won't last long in any league. You need the ability to remain cool under pressure. Often, games are played in front of large crowds, and fans can be vocal in their criticism of players, coaches, and especially sports officials.

You must also have a thorough understanding of the sport you officiate. You need to be informed about changes to the rules. Sports officials keep informed by attending clinics and seminars sponsored by professional associations.

EXPLORING

A great way to find out if you enjoy being an umpire or referee is to officiate for a Little League team or at a summer camp. Try to locate a sports official in your area and set up an interview. Also, you should continue to watch and participate in sports to learn more.

EMPLOYERS

There are approximately 16,000 sports officials employed in this field. Sports officials are employed by professional and semiprofessional leagues, sports organizations, youth leagues, and schools at all levels.

STARTING OUT

A person interested in becoming a referee or umpire should begin officiating Little League or amateur league games on weekends and at night. You may even want to volunteer your time. For a paid position, beginners need to pass a written examination and join the state association of officials for each sport they choose to officiate.

ADVANCEMENT

The natural progression for umpires and referees is to begin by officiating young peoples' games and advance to amateur adults' contests. Those with talent and determination may move on to college games or professional minor leagues.

Many officials who would like to move to the professional level attend umpire or referee camps. Many of these camps are conducted by actual professional officials. These programs feature a rigorous review of rules and regulations and often include game situations.

The minor leagues in baseball are a testing ground for prospective umpires. On average, umpires spend six to eight years at the minor-league level before they are even considered for a major-league position. Football officials must have 10 years of officiating experience, five years of which must have been at a collegiate varsity or minor professional level, before they can work in the NFL.

EARNINGS

Umpire and referee salaries vary greatly, depending on the sport and the level at which it is played. Typically, the closer an official gets to the top of a professional sports league, the higher the wages, but this is not always the case. For example, some college basketball referees might earn more money than a non-lead official in a less popular professional sport.

The U.S. Department of Labor reports that umpires, referees, and related sports officials had median annual earnings of $22,880 in 2006. Salaries ranged from less than $14,120 to more than $45,430. According to the Major League Baseball's Umpire Development Program, umpire salaries range from $1,800 to $2,000 per month in the Rookie League to $2,500 to $3,400 per month in the triple-A league to a starting annual salary of approximately $120,000 for a major-league umpire. Major-league umpires with considerable experience can earn as much as $350,000 a year. Professional basketball officials' salaries range from approximately $85,000 to $300,000, depending on the experience of the official.

Officials in the National Football League are considered part-time employees. They earn salaries that range from approximately $29,000 to $100,000.

In professional sports, umpires and referees are typically given additional money for travel, hotel, and food expenses. These officials also receive extra payment if they are invited to work special events such as the World Series or Stanley Cup Finals. Football officials who work the Super Bowl, for example, are paid approximately $12,000.

Umpires and referees at the college, amateur, and youth levels are paid by the game. College officials earn between $200 and $800 per game, and high school and middle school officials earn considerably less. The Arizona State Interscholastic Athletic Commission, for example, cites officials' earnings as approximately $19 to $25 per game, depending on the sport.

WORK ENVIRONMENT

Professional officials work in front of huge crowds. Their judgments and decisions are scrutinized by the fans in the stadium and by millions of fans watching at home.

Professional football officials work one game a week, while baseball umpires may work up to six games a week. Some football stadiums are outdoors, and football officials may have to work through inclement weather. Baseball umpires may work outside also, but they can stop the game because of rain.

Being an official at any level can be stressful. Officials must make split-second, unbiased decisions. Rulings are bound to be unpopular, at least to the team or player that is penalized, and even an eight-year-old Little Leaguer can be quite vocal.

Professional officials travel extensively throughout the season. They may be away from home for weeks at a time. Airplane flights, hotel food, and living out of a suitcase are some of the things that professional sports officials must endure.

At any level and with any sport, the work can be physically demanding. Baseball umpires must crouch behind the catcher to call balls and strikes. Basketball referees must run up and down the court, just as hockey officials must skate the rink. Football officials run the risk of colliding with heavily protected, helmeted players.

However, if a person enjoys travel and can withstand the verbal abuse from players, coaches, and fans, the job can be very rewarding. Actual hours spent officiating are relatively short. The duration of most games is less than three hours.

Many people become officials because they enjoy sports. When an athlete's playing days are over, becoming an official is one way to maintain an active and important role in the sporting world. Most high school and junior high umpires and referees will tell you that they officiate not for the money, but because they enjoy it.

OUTLOOK

The growth outlook for the field of sports officiating depends on the sport and the league worked. Umpires and referees are almost always needed at the youth, high school, and amateur levels, and people who are interested in supplementing their incomes this way or simply learning about the field of officiating should find plenty of opportunities for work, especially part-time work.

In professional sports the market is much tighter. Umpires in the major leagues rarely leave the job except to retire. In fact, during a 10-year period, the American League hired only three new umpires. When an opening does occur, an umpire moves up from triple-A baseball, creating an opening for an umpire from double-A, and so on. Professional sports without minor leagues offer even fewer employment opportunities for officials at the professional level. The creation of new leagues and expansion teams does occasionally offer additional job opportunities for professional sports officials.

The outlook for women sports officials has improved in recent years with the creation of women's professional basketball leagues such as the WNBA, offering many new positions to women officials, as well as coaches, trainers, and professional athletes. Additionally, in 1997, two women, Dee Kantner and Violet Palmer, became the first female referees to officiate NBA basketball games—a first for the all-male U.S. major sports leagues. Perhaps, in the future, more openings for women officials will be created as the other leagues follow suit.

FOR MORE INFORMATION

Visit the association's Web site for information on careers in baseball umpiring and to participate in an online forum.
Association of Minor League Umpires
PO Box 1571
Andover, MA 01810-0027
Email: amlu@amlu.org
http://www.amlu.org

For information on training schools, requirements, and other information for becoming a basketball official, contact
International Association of Approved Basketball Officials
PO Box 1300
Germantown, MD 20875-1300
Tel: 301-540-5180
http://www.iaabo.org

The following professional umpiring schools are recognized by Major League Baseball for the Umpire Development Program:
Harry Wendelstedt School for Umpires
88 South Saint Andrews Drive
Ormond Beach, FL 32174-3857
Tel: 386-672-4879
Email: admin@umpireschool.com
http://www.umpireschool.com

Jim Evans Academy of Professional Umpiring
200 South Wilcox Street, #508
Castle Rock, CO 80104-1913
Tel: 303-290-7411
Email: jimsacademy@earthlink.net
http://www.umpireacademy.com

Contact the NASO for information on sports officials' camps and clinics and becoming a sports official. The association also publishes Becoming a Sports Official *and* Referee Magazine.
National Association of Sports Officials (NASO)
2017 Lathrop Avenue
Racine, WI 53405-3758
Tel: 262-632-5448
Email: naso@naso.org
http://www.naso.org

Visit the association's Web site for information on union representation for Major League Baseball umpires, training opportunities, and interesting facts about umpires.
World Umpires Association
PO Box 394
Neenah, WI 54957-0394
http://www.worldumpires.com

The following Web site offers links to amateur and professional baseball umpiring associations throughout the world:
John Skilton's Baseball Links
http://www.baseball-links.com

To learn more about professional baseball umpiring camps, visit
Major League Baseball Umpire Camps
http://mlb.mlb.com/mlb/official_info/umpires/camp/index.jsp

For a wealth of information on baseball umpiring, including how to become an umpire, rules and measurements of the game, FAQs, and A Step-by-Step Guide on Becoming an Umpire, *visit*
Major League Baseball: Umpires
http://www.mlb.com/NASApp/mlb/mlb/official_info/mlb_umpires.jsp

Index

Entries in **boldface** indicate main articles.

A

AAASP. *See* Association for the Advancement of Applied Sports Psychology

AAHPERD. *See* American Alliance for Health, Physical Education, Recreation and Dance

AASP. *See* Association for Applied Sport Psychology

ABCA. *See* American Baseball Coaches Association

administrative assistants 63

AEMA. *See* Athletic Equipment Managers Association

Affirmed (horse) 24

Agence France-Presse 173

agents. *See* sports agents; sports publicists

Alcott, Amy 34

AMA. *See* American Medical Association

Amateur Athletic Union 41, 51

American Alliance for Health, Physical Education, Recreation and Dance (AAHPERD) 41, 51, 129

American Baseball Coaches Association (ABCA) 129

American Board of Orthopaedic Surgery 137

American College of Sports Medicine 141, 170

American Football Coaches Association 129

American Hockey Coaches Association 129

American Institute of Architects 110–111

American Medical Association (AMA) 141, 163

American Orthopaedic Society for Sports Medicine 141

American Psychological Association (APA) 61, 63–64, 68

American Society for Horticultural Science 21

American Society of Exercise Physiologists (ASEP) 166, 167

American Sportscasters Association 87

American Statistical Association 161

American Telephone and Telegraph (AT&T) 79

anchors 82. *See also* sports broadcasters

announcers. *See* sports announcers

Anson, Cap 147

APA. *See* American Psychological Association

Arcaro, Eddie 24

Architect Registration Examination 106

architects 102. *See also* sports facility designers

Arena Football League 97, 142

arena managers 112. *See also* sports facility managers

arenas 102

Aristotle 131, 162

Arizona State Interscholastic Athletic Commission 194

arthroscopic surgery 133

ASEP. *See* American Society of Exercise Physiologists

assemblers 54. *See also* sporting goods production workers

assistant coaches 149. *See also* coaches; sports scouts

Associated Press 80, 173
Sports Editors 177, 180
Woman Athlete of the Year 34

associate editors 179. *See also* sportswriters

Association for the Advancement of Applied Sports Psychology (AAASP) 64

Association for Applied Sport Psychology (AASP) 62, 68, 69

Association for Women in Sports Media (AWSM) 87, 180

Association of Collegiate Schools of Architecture 109, 111

Association of Minor League Umpires 195

Association of Racing Commissioners International 27

athletes 132. *See also* female athletes; professional athletes–individual sports; professional athletes–team sports

Athletic Equipment Managers Association (AEMA) 89–90, 91, 93–94

athletic trainers. *See* sports trainers

AT&T. *See* American Telephone and Telegraph

AWSM. *See* Association for Women in Sports Media

B

Babylon 14, 23, 153

ball assemblers 54. *See also* sporting goods production workers

baseball
development of 53
equipment 54–55
major leagues 44
popularity of 43
professional athletes—team sports 1, 33, 42, 44
umpires 189, 192. *See also* umpires

baseball announcers 82. *See also* sports announcers

baseball glove shapers 55. *See also* sporting goods production workers

base umpires 189. *See also* umpires

basketball
development of 52
equipment 53, 54
female athletes 34
popularity of 43
professional athletes—team sports 1, 33, 42, 44
referees 189, 193–194. *See also* referees

Becoming a Sports Official 196

Belmont Stakes 24

bench assemblers 53. *See also* sporting goods production workers